SAFE PASSAGE: TRAVELS THROUGH
THE TWENTIETH CENTURY

SAFE PASSAGE

TRAVELS THROUGH
THE TWENTIETH CENTURY

Donald MacKay

ROBIN BRASS STUDIO

Published 2010 by Robin Brass Studio Inc.
www.rbstudiobooks.com

ISBN-13: 978-1-896941-61-5
ISBN-10: 1-896941-61-3

Printed and bound in Canada by Marquis Imprimeur Inc., Cap-Saint-Ignace, Quebec

Library and Archives Canada Cataloguing in Publication

MacKay, Donald, 1925-
    Safe passage : travels through the twentieth century / Donald MacKay.

Includes index.
ISBN 978-1-896941-61-5

1. MacKay, Donald, 1925– . 2. Journalists – Canada – Biography. 3. Foreign correspondents – Canada – Biography. I. Title.

PN4913.M39A3 2010   070.4'332092   C2010-900795-6

For Barbara, Marina, Karen,
Siân and Matthew,
with love.

CONTENTS

"Life must move forward, but can only be understood backward." Søren Kierkegaard

1

CLOSING THE CIRCLE

While trying to divert my mind from minor surgery in the Annapolis Valley Hospital not long ago, treacherous memory carried me back sixty-five years, almost to the day, to a more serious occasion. I had lain on a white table here before.

That earlier encounter had begun in wartime Halifax. LeMarchant Street School having closed for the summer of 1941, my friend Bob Knight and I had lied about our ages and had summer jobs manhandling munitions for the Royal Canadian Army Ordnance Corps. We were playing soccer with some soldiers in a dusty field during lunch break when I began coughing up surprisingly bright red blood. There had been no warning. With aching head I walked my bike across the city to south-end Seymour Street.

No one was at home so I lay on my bed and tried to read. Although more important things have disappeared down my memory hole, I remember the book, *The Cloister and the Hearth,* Charles Reade's medieval adventure novel. I never did finish it. My mother came home from the marine shipping company where she worked and summoned our aging family doctor. Four months earlier he had ascribed my occasional cough and loss of weight to teenage growing pains. Those being the days of house calls, he came that night and tapped my chest, took my soaring temperature, told me I was lucky the hemorrhage hadn't killed me and diagnosed pulmonary tuberculosis, my right lung having been weakened by pneumonia when I was twelve. Nova Scotia had the highest TB mortality rate in the nation and my Aunt Norma, who taught piano lessons and kept a white bust of Schubert on her mantle, embarrassed me by weeping

I

at my bedside, convinced I was bound for teenage heaven.

Tuberculosis is a treatable disease but I had caught it before strep-
tomycin appeared and when it was as fearsome as leprosy, and more
infectious. My mother sensibly whisked me off to the Nova Scotia
Sanatorium, which stood on the pine-clad hill above the town of
Kentville where the Annapolis Valley Hospital now stands. A scary
consultation of four doctors prescribed bed rest, fresh air and a process called artificial pneumothorax, which temporarily collapsed my
right lung to give it a chance to heal, a treatment so ancient it was
described by Hippocrates 2400 years ago. Nostrums over the centuries have included a poultice of garlic and dog fat, seaweed "placed
under the bed," or my favourite, which was the leisurely South Seas
voyage recommended to Robert Louis Stevenson. Instead of joining
grade ten that autumn I entered the Nova Scotia Sanatorium on
July 14, 1941, three days before my sixteenth birthday, and remained
nine months in an institutional time warp until I was allowed to go
home to convalesce for two years and acquire some self-administered
education.

A few weeks before my eighteenth birthday I had a lucky break
which put me on the road to the career I was to follow for thirty-
two years. I landed an editorial job at the Canadian Press bureau in
Halifax because all the qualified people had joined the military. I
stayed a year, but as the sententious Dr. Samuel Johnson declared,
"Every man thinks meanly of himself for not having been a soldier and not having been at sea," although in fact Dr. Johnson had
been neither. The armed forces having turned me down, I joined the
Merchant Navy and was apprenticed to the Norwegian oil tanker
M/T *Peik*, which took me to wartime Britain, Norway, Denmark
and Germany.

After the war I left Nova Scotia – forever I thought – and lived
in Montreal, Toronto, Winnipeg, Vancouver, Manhattan, London,
Lisbon, Munich and rural Ireland and reported news from Canada,

Europe, West Africa, India and China. Now, in the early years of the 21st century, I was back, a white-haired octogenarian victim of nostalgia, which my dictionary calls "a sentimental yearning for a return to some real or romanticized setting in the past."

Halifax in my absence had become more real than romantic. The city where I'd grown up had escaped its narrow, hilly peninsula, two miles wide and seven miles long, and thrust suburbs into the rock-ribbed county, quadrupled its size and altered its personality. It was crowded, boisterous, multicultural, newly-cosmopolitan, with five universities, fine dining, bars and pubs like "The Liquor Dome," and suburban shopping malls which sucked the life out of old business districts like Barrington Street. The overtly teetotal city I had known, in which there were bootleggers but no legal pubs or bars and hardly any restaurants or night life, now claimed more jazz joints and bars per capita than almost any other city in Canada. High-rise buildings, which tend to make all cities look alike, towered above streets of two-storey wooden houses and the Old Town Clock, which has been ticking for over two centuries. Museums, gift shops, restaurants and huge container ships had reclaimed the waterfront from rusty tramp freighters and salty fishing schooners. People referred to something called "HRM," which I discovered had nothing to do with royalty as I first thought but meant the new Halifax Regional Municipality, which awkwardly embraced a county as big as the province of Prince Edward Island so that only people with houses on the peninsula lived in the real Halifax. When I was a young reporter two murders a year constituted a crime wave. Now there were many, and drug wars, muggings and holdups. Halifax had changed. The city still smelt of the sea when the east wind was blowing but Halifax was no longer home.

It was out on the back roads among the white farm houses, wrap-around porches, red barns, fields, rivers, hills and mayflowers that I found the province I had known. Sparsely-populated, lake-dotted

Nova Scotia is one place, like Quebec, where people from Europe had lived longest on this land and learned to become Canadians. The names are Mi'kmaq, English, Scottish, French and Irish: Mushaboom, Kraut Point, Main a Dieu, Shag Harbour, Malignant Cove, Burnt Coat, Ecum Secum, Lower Economy, Skunk Hole, Sodom Lake, Portapique, Slobbery Meadow, The Devils Burrow, and Melancholy Mountain, where the lost children died in 1841.

On this quasi-island, joined so tentatively to the rest of Canada by a narrow marshy isthmus, nowhere is far from the sea. South along Lighthouse Trail the islands are a scattered jigsaw puzzle. On roads where I'd once biked and hitchhiked and slept in itchy hay lofts the sun sparkles on blue coves and green headlands: on Chester, an opulent green town of white houses and white sails; on Mahone Bay's timeless illusion of perfection; on salty Lunenburg and Captains Courageous braving the Grand Banks in wind-driven schooners. The cod are gone but men still fish out of foggy Bacarro, named for monster codfish caught in Elizabethan times by fishermen from Portugal, Spain and England. Shelburne, where Loyalists in 1783 failed to build the biggest town in British North America, remains a living footnote to history favoured by movie directors seeking atmosphere. Down at Church Point, the biggest wooden church in the world looms out of the fog, a great white Acadian Catholic whale of a building with bronze bells cast in France.

North across the spine of the province – hills, bogs, gnawed-over forests of hardwoods and Christmas trees, lakes, lonely settlements – lies the old town of Windsor, where I lived the first thirteen years of my life and with the scenery-blindness of the young failed to notice the beauty of the hills which enclose the town in a wide green bowl. Windsor, like Halifax, has changed. From afar Windsor's church steeples and leafy trees may look like rural England but at its business core many handsome Edwardian brick business buildings have disappeared, victims of a suburban mall. The Avon River which had

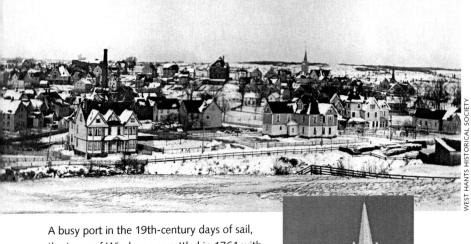

A busy port in the 19th-century days of sail, the town of Windsor was settled in 1764 with a thriving economy based on farming. The Baptist church (right), from which I resigned at the age of eight, was one of half a dozen places of worship in a town of 3,000 people.

WEST HANTS HISTORICAL SOCIETY

washed its muddy bed with tremendous tides twice a day had mysteriously vanished. Wilson's drug store, where I'd spent my weekly allowance on chocolate rosebuds and Tiptop Comics, had also disappeared along with Doran's tobacco shop, where Ken Ritchie did magic tricks with cards and eggs and sold cigars to commercial travellers who read the *Halifax Herald* on the veranda of the red-brick Victoria Hotel. The travellers arrived on a train driven by my grandfather that rumbled and whistled through town in a shroud of steam, hot oil and coal smoke. A causeway bearing a highway now severs Windsor's river from the sea.

The tall haunted house at Gerrish and King, which at the age of seven I'd hurried by for fear the street light would reveal a goblin face peering down from an attic window, is now a harmless senior citizens home. The brick post office with its lighted clock tower has been replaced by a functional little impostor, and Bustin's Imperial

Gerrish Street, Windsor, in 1927, two years after I was born. Model T Fords coexisted with horses and buggies.

Theatre, with its gleaming 1930s restaurant, is headquarters of Mermaid Theatre, the international puppet company. Gone is the Opera House where I appeared in bathrobe and towel-turban in a nativity play and again in dunce cap and black clown suit sprinkled with the white musical note "Doh."

Since the places of our childhood exist in time rather than space, the brown, wooden two-storey home of my MacRae grandparents where I had spent early years has nothing now to say to me. It has shrunk. But the little canary-yellow house where I'd later lived with my mother on King Street shook up a kaleidoscope of memories. Some were as simple as a game of marbles beside April mud puddles which reflected white clouds, others were as mysterious as an autumn car ride with my mother through a dark countryside to a big white tent lit by oil lamps and smelling of kerosene and the charred wood of what must have been a burnt farm house. Some images were black

6

and white and fragmentary, others as clear as coloured photographs.

Born in the Roaring Twenties, the age of flappers, the Charleston, the invention of sliced bread and bubble gum, I remember horses and oxen with brass ornaments sharing the streets with Model T Fords. Of all senses, smell can be the most evocative, and Sunday mornings smelt of shoe polish and mothballs, and Christmas of oranges and cinnamon. I remember the musky feed grain, barrels of apples, tarred rope and turpentine in the brick warehouse on Water Street where my mother was office manager. Every autumn she kept the accounts of the Hants County Exhibition, where I had free entry to a world of cattle, sheep, straw, hay, bruised grass, noise and the glamorous excitement of the tawdry fairground: perilous Midway rides, thumping caliopes, frying onions, spun sugar and the dim and musty interiors of dubious sideshow tents.

My eighty-year-old copy of McAlpine's Gazetteer, which is nearly as old as I am, reminds me of how much in the Annapolis Valley has changed. Apple Blossom Queens are still crowned every spring, though the apple is no longer king and Nova Scotia has become a land of grapes and wineries for the first time since Pierre Martin planted the first apple seeds in 1663.

Gone are the cider mills, barrel makers, harness shops, blacksmiths and the general store selling groceries, lanterns, ox whips, brooms, dresses, patent medicines and dishes printed with roses. Thriving crossroad communities have been reduced to a church and a graveyard. One of the last covered bridges (which lulled farm animals into sensing they were entering a barn rather than crossing a river) was at Grand Pré near Wolfville; as a homesick ten-year-old spending a summer away from my mother with an elderly farm couple, I helped harvest marsh hay, driving a red, horse-drawn rake on dikeland rescued from the sea by doomed eighteenth-century Acadians who had forgotten France. It was here in 1755 Acadians were rounded up in a brutal ethnic cleansing and shipped to southern

Cape Blomidon changes with the seasons, rosy-red and green in summer, grey in autumn mist, white and green in winter. In Mi'kmaq legend it is the home of the godly Glooscap who created mankind from an ash tree and rode on the backs of whales.

American states, their rich farmlands soon occupied by land-hungry New Englanders.

Before coming home I'd read two books which prompted my return: Ernest Buckler's *The Mountain and the Valley*, a novel by a kinder, gentler Thomas Hardy, and Harold Horwood's nature study of the Annapolis Basin, *Dancing on the Shore*, a poetic reminder that all living creatures are fellow travellers in a finite world. Both men, not much older than I, are dead. And now late in the day and late in life, coming over the hills to my new home in the hill-side university town of Wolfville, I saw Cape Blomidon, a small magic mountain of rosy sandstone and forest green looming across the Fundy tides as in my home thoughts from abroad.

When I was a child Blomidon crouched in the distance like a friendly giant, not letting me out of sight. "It is the first thing we look for when we are returning home," wrote the Acadia University professor Esther Clark Wright. "We love it in somewhat the way we love a grandparent, because it had a part in making us what we are." The Nova Scotia-born diplomat Charles Ritchie, enchanted by Wolfville's white houses and rose gardens, wrote, "The little town seems like a place met at the beginning of a fairy story, before out-of-the-way things start to happen." What sort of fairy tales – sad, dark or happy – he did not linger to discover.

Novelists taking their cue from Psalm 90-9 suggest a suitable way of accounting for one's life is by treating it as a story. But what sort of story? A memoir can obviously be distorted by time and imagination, but in the end memory defines us all; my own memory seems to contain more fact than fiction although it grows less linear and more circular with the years. Which is why my homecoming after long absence evoked questions. Why was my name missing from among my classmates in the records of Windsor Academy? Why was my grandmother's rich uncle named Gotobed?

Bigger questions too: As my passport states, I was born in the obscure hamlet of East Portapique, of which I know little apart from that Acadian pioneers named it for the porcupine and it was near the childhood home of the American Poet Laureate Elizabeth Bishop. What my passport does not state is that I was born in a rural post office. Why East Portapique? Why a post office? And what happened to the father I never knew?

2

AMBIGUOUS BEGINNINGS

"Backward, turn backward, O Time, in your flight /
Make me a child again, just for tonight!" E.A. Allen

One July evening in 1928 a stranger came to visit. He was tall
and indistinct and helped me with my buttons when I had to
go to bed. I was three years old. They said the visitor was my father,
but I never saw him again.

William Glenthorne MacKay and Dorothy Agnes MacRae, both
twenty-two, were married February 20, 1925, in Windsor, Nova Scotia, although their marriage certificate bears a confusing second date
which suggests they were married the previous February. I suspect
that second date was wishful thinking by the Baptist minister who
signed the certificate. My birth date was July 17, 1925, which mutely
suggests why I saw the light of day in the hamlet of East Portapique,
Colchester County, rather than the cottage hospital in Windsor,
Hants County.

The night I was born my mother's little sister Gwendolyn, known
for some reason as Bertie, ran through the spruce woods to fetch the
doctor to our cousin's farmhouse, which doubled as rural post office.
A photo reveals a plump, dimpled, grinning "Billie MacKay, Dot's
Boy" and on the back is written "He is so cute I should keep him,
but thot the family would like him around, Love Edna." That was
a nice thought by my Cousin Edna, but my mother took me to live
with the MacRaes in Windsor. I'd been christened William Donald
and was sometimes called Junior but after my father disappeared to
California I was Donald or Don.

Just why young Dorothy and Bill, a railway engineer's daughter fresh from business school and a bank clerk from New Glasgow, where his father was railway station agent, separated after such a short marriage I can only guess. They've been dead these many years but were young in the Roaring Twenties when even small towns felt the liberating fizz of the Jazz Age and women learned to smoke and dance the Charleston. Dorothy was an attractive, dark haired, poetry-loving romantic and Bill was a lonely young man

"Dot's Boy," the traveller, at the age of one, 1926.

in a strange town. I imagine he must have been given a rough time by Dorothy's father, a self-made, upwardly mobile man of uncertain background in an unforgiving small town where divorce was rare and probably shameful.

My mother did not seek a divorce for twenty years and then only when she remarried; she had destroyed all photos of my father and never mentioned him, which come to think of it was not a good idea so far as I was concerned but it didn't concern me at the time. Long after his death, and hers, his sister in Montreal showed me a photo: a slim, greying, grey-suited man with an apologetic smile, holding a grey fedora. I had become the father of two children myself by then and the photo evoked nothing more than curiosity as to what this man could have been thinking when he left us. I was living in Europe in the 1950s when I heard he'd settled in Ontario with a new wife and my half-sister, whom I've never met. He died in his fifties and when I

William Glenthorne MacKay, who died in his mid-fifties – my sole photograph of the father I never knew.

came across his obituary I saw it made no mention of me, which made me feel odd. I suppose perceived parental rejection can be a lifelong source of anxiety, but I've heard that if a child is blessed with one good parent it suffers no lasting harm. At all events I've never been sure what effect, if any, Bill's defection has had on my life.

My mother earned our living doing secretarial or accounting work, including a year in "the Boston States" when I was five; it was my grandmother Pearl, then in her fifties and more pal than granny, who nursed me through colds, mumps, measles, scarlet fever and chicken pox. I called her Mum for the reason I called my mother Dot, because everyone else did. My real mother was never demonstratively loving but she did her best, supporting us both by her secretarial and accounting skills when women were ill-paid and vulnerable. She was bookish, wrote romantic unpublished poems and short stories and gave me a great gift, a love of literature. She died at the age of eighty-two before I could thank her in the way I would like to now.

The MacRaes of Gerrish Street included an uncle young enough to be my brother and four aunts who bought me books to match my changing years: *The Child's Garden of Verse, Winnie the Pooh, The Wind in the Willows, The Books of Knowledge, Uncle Remus, Alice in Wonderland, The Wizard of Oz, Boy's Own Annual, Treasure Island.* They introduced me to music in a home where everyone sang and

Dorothy Agnes MacKay, a single mother who raised a son in an unenlight-
ened age when women in business faced serious gender bias. She died in
hospital at age eighty-two.

played an instrument. The MacRaes in those days attended the
Baptist Church, which I quit at age eight, forsaking belief in a life
hereafter and the obvious social benefits of church-going when faced
with total immersion in a tin tub sunk in the church floor and that
creepy, lugubrious, hymn "Just as I am, without one plea," which
accompanied baptism. Although unsure whether I had a soul, I was
content there was no medieval heaven above the clouds or hell in the

(Right to left) Grandmother Pearl MacRae, Great-grandmother Isadora McCully and Great-aunt Hill, affectionately known as "Ant Hill." For Uncle John and myself the MacRae house on Gerrish Street often seemed a matriarchy.

underground depths below. In later years when I lived among other cultures, I found better reasons for the road I had taken, including a year studying comparative religions, Hinduism, Buddhism and Islam. Only once, twenty years later while reporting a religious event in Barcelona, was I momentarily tempted to join a church. I see no reason to do so now in my old age. I shall always, however, be keenly interested in the great religions which all began when mankind began to grow more civilized in "the axis age" between 800 and 200 BC.

My grandmother held the household together while my grandfather drove the steam trains of the Dominion Atlantic Railway, having worked his way up from chore boy and engine wiper. A member of the Masonic Lodge and an autodidact, Jack MacRae spent his free time in his study, which smelled of pipe tobacco and books. He gave me a red fire engine and a tall rocking horse one Christmas, but I had a sense he would rather I wasn't there. I remember no spankings, but my grandfather once gave me a kick with his slipper for leaving the telephone off the hook. I was indignant at the time, but realise now his ire was prompted by the need to keep an open phone line because of his job as a train driver on call.

My grandmother was the friendly one. People of many shapes and sizes and several colours would come and sit in the corner of the kitchen by the wood box while Dickey sang in his cage. An elderly relative named Walter, who wore a railway conductor's uniform, gave me a sample of his chewing tobacco, which made me sick. A young politician smelling of shaving lotion and cigars came to court one of my aunts and stayed to fix my fire engine. There was a mysterious black man named Coalfleet who, I was told, had been rescued as a baby from a coal barge by Pearl's sea captain grandfather. It was in the kitchen I met my first Indian. Twice a month Mrs. Maloney, a stout Mi'kmaq from Shubenacadie came on the Midland Railway train and perfumed the kitchen with sweet grass from the woven baskets she'd come to sell. I remember the sights, sounds and particularly the new smells of my first rail journey in 1930 when I was five. The Great Depression hardly affected us because my grandfather had a railway job, although I developed a strong aversion to wasting food. Occasionally, young men who rode the rails looking for work picking apples knocked on our back door and were fed in the kitchen with sandwiches and soup.

My grandmother's mother, Isadora McCully, née Faulkner, thin as a witch and not five feet tall, lived next door. Daughter of a sailing ship captain from down-river Hantsport, she had been orphaned, we were told, by a "plague" caused by decaying pilot whales washed ashore. She was adopted by the Churchill shipbuilding family, whose home is now a museum, and married railway conductor George McCully, a relative of Judge Jonathan McCully, a Father of Confederation. George's uncle was T.G. (Thomas Gotobed) McMullen of Truro, "Lumber King of Nova Scotia" and the elected member for

Colchester County. McMullen owned a saw mill, leased or owned 300,000 acres of woodland, exported lumber to England on three sailing ships and built the fifty-mile Midland Railway between Truro and Windsor. I was disappointed to learn "Gotobed" was the surname of his north of England relatives and not an injunction carried over from childhood. Isadora called me Bug and fed me peppermints though I suspect she disliked little boys. Clad to her heels in black bombazine and a polka-dot blue apron, she forgot her terrible arthritis one morning and chased me around the garden with a wicked paring knife because I had snatched, for the third and last time, a handful of the garden peas she had been fretfully shelling.

Apart from a mahogany wind-up gramophone we had a big cabinet radio in the "front room" and my favourite programs were *Jack Armstrong, The All American Boy, The Lone Ranger, Little Orphan Annie, Buck Rogers in the 25th Century,* and, later, *The Shadow* ("What evil lurks in the hearts of men – The Shadow Knows"). But for many years the most exciting room in the Gerrish Street house had been the attic crammed with discarded toys, nineteenth-century clothes useful for play acting on rainy days, flags, bunting, memorabilia of Queen Victoria's Jubilee, the Boer war, World War I, and a magic lantern with slides of the Holy Land. The railway-red barn behind the house where a pony once lived had an acrid smell from the rat-plagued hen house. On the top floor someone had fashioned a gym with punching bag and trapeze where my grandparents Pearl and Jack were reputed to have donned boxing gloves occasionally for some alternative marital sport.

My mother had a difficult time getting me to begin school in 1931 at the age of six. On my first day I told the teacher my name was David, probably because I liked that name better than my own. David remained in those yellowing attendance books, which was why, I discovered a lifetime later, I failed to find my name among my schoolmates. Windsor Academy, which no longer exists, smelt of

At fifty feet, some of the highest tides in the world left shipping on the Avon River at Windsor immobilized high and dry for several hours every day.

(Below) Down-river at Hantsport in 1888 stranded but unburied pilot whales, which farmers unwisely had used for fertilizer, caused "blackfish cholera," which killed thirty-four residents, including my great-great-grandparents.

children, chalk dust, the dank, dark basement where the toilets were, and the industrial-strength perfume of Miss Sweet, who looked a bit like Popeye's Olive Oyle and introduced my hand to the strap. I never liked school, though in grade three I fell in love with young Miss Brown, who rewarded me with first prize, a foot-long pencil shaped like a cane, for a poem called "The Mouse" inspired by Robert Burns. She left to marry a teacher whom I felt unworthy of her.

In summers when child-time stretched forever, I swam in warm milk-chocolate-brown pools among mudflats in the Avon River after the fifty-foot tides gushed out to the sea twice a day. When I got home I was smeared with mud picked up as I ran for the shore to escape the tidal wall of water surging back up the river. Sailing ships carrying potatoes and coal tied up along Water Street, where steam trains driven by my grandfather thundered through town on the way down the Valley to Yarmouth. (All that's left of our rushing, muddy river now is a timid freshwater lagoon.)

At dawn one July morning I pulled on a white shirt, tan shorts and ratty brown sneakers and ran down King Street hill to watch elephants step gingerly off a train while the faded big top slowly rose like a monstrous brown mushroom. I went fishing down beyond the railroad among the dikes and fields a mile or so from our house. One day when I was ten I caught two fish and was walking home across the fields when I saw two older boys who I knew as bullies coming toward me. They caught me at one of the fences, stole my fish and beat me up. I promised myself I'd get even but never did. During recess one morning in grade five I fought another bully, a farmer's son who wore lumbermen's rubbers and overalls and smelled of manure. The teacher sent me home to change my bloody shirt. On Saturday afternoons we re-enacted Tom Mix, Buck Jones and Tarzan movies, which we'd seen for ten cents in Bustin's Imperial Theatre. One of my friends was a dark-haired, fatherless girl of my own age whose brother was serving a term in Dorchester penitentiary. I'd regarded her as a tomboy until one day, alone in her mother's kitchen, we started kissing, one thing led to another, and she whispered the two most suggestive two words I'd ever heard and I froze. We were around ten or eleven years old. Instead of sampling pre-teen sex I swore off girls and went riding around the countryside on my liberating blue CCF bicycle, feeling a little guilty at having abandoned her. In autumn I played rugby and joined a gym and hunted inoffensive small creatures in the woods with my single-shot air gun and dreamed of the .22 rifle that lived in the window of the hardware store.

Having learned the joys of tennis at the age of nine, summers seemed to stretch forever. There were always things to do and on rainy days one could curl up with a book at my grandmother's house in the cosy little second-floor den overlooking busy Gerrish Street.

In April 1936 I was walking past the fire hall when I heard through an open window a broadcast from Nova Scotia's Moose River gold mine. Claustrophobic mine rescues were always headline news but this was different: live broadcast journalism of the sort introduced in the United States only two years later. I no longer dreamed of being a Mountie or driving Dink Mounce's yellow steam engine which rolled the tarmac. I would become a reporter.

My favourite subjects were English, history and marching and drilling to the bugles and drums of the cadet corps, where I was sergeant major because I was big for my age, could shout clear orders and had a clean uniform my grandmother kept pressed. I joined the Boy Scouts and their world of knots, hikes and wilderness camps at Murphy Lake, where we nailed sleeping platforms high in the spruce trees and played a night game in which half the boys defended a steep hill on which a lone candle burned while the other half crept up through the dark to snuff it out and win the game.

I was not quite thirteen the Saturday night four of us boys left Windsor at ten o'clock to ride our bicycles some forty miles down dark gravel roads to Williams Lake. We left late because one of the group had to work until ten in a grocery store. We arrived at dawn to join ten thousand people in hundreds of white tents. In the week of the August moon, professional hunting guides from all over Canada and the United States had gathered as they did every year to compete

in rifle shooting, fly casting, canoe racing, portaging, log burling, log chopping, moose calling and cooking pancakes and bacon over camp fires. It was my last Windsor adventure before my mother, age thirty-six and wanting more from life than a small town had to offer, moved us seventy miles to Halifax.

Twenty years after World War I and three before the start of World War II, army cadet corps, complete with heavy rifles and bugle bands, were popular in the schools.

3

A KIND OF EDUCATION

In the long, sunny summer of 1938 the city of Halifax was dozing through the Great Depression. Fireweed sprouted in waterfront railway sidings, Georgian buildings were quietly mouldering on Hollis Street and few ships came to the port whose destiny since its founding in 1749 had been to serve Britain in wartime and rusticate in time of peace

There were lingering traces of the era when imperial Halifax was the grandest British base in the Americas with a harbour full of tall ships and the hill-top Citadel crawling with redcoats. From Halifax young James Wolfe, the dauntless hero who had won his spurs at the brutal massacre of Bonny Prince Charlie's Scots at Culloden, sailed up the St. Lawrence in 1759 to triumph and death at Quebec; from Halifax General Robert Ross sailed in the summer of 1814 to burn down the Washington White House in revenge, it was said, for the American raid on the site that became Toronto. From Privateers Wharf on Water Street legalized pirates authorized by His Majesty plundered foreign vessels for the booty which financed Nova Scotia's first bank.

Their ghosts were not forgotten. In 1938 military bands still played "Rule Britannia" and the noon gun boomed on Citadel Hill as it did when Queen Victoria's father commanded the garrison. With a population of 60,000 my boyhood Halifax fitted snugly into its boot-shaped little peninsula between the harbour to the east and the Atlantic's Northwest Arm. The lime-green Atlantic with its promise of voyages was an exciting revelation for me, who had learned to swim in the opaque muddy tidal pools of the river, so unlike

Named for the enterprising George Montagu-Dunk, 18th-century president of the British Board of Trade and Plantations, 2nd Earl of Halifax, the old port had a history of wartime boom and peacetime gloom. In this view from the 1960s by Nova Scotia artist Latham B. Jenson, the city is little changed since my teenage years there. (Courtesy Alma Jenson)

Shakespeare's Avon, at Windsor, Nova Scotia. My playgrounds encompassed the woodland acres of seaside Point Pleasant Park with its Martello Tower (built to guard Halifax from Napoleon) and the fishy wharfs where during the Depression I learned to pour hot water into empty Caribbean rum hogsheads to produce an unpleasantly wishy-washy drink called "swish." "Haligonians share a secret," wrote Halifax-lover Harry Bruce of his adopted city, "and the secret is the sea … it shapes the city's character." I guess it shaped mine.

My mother found work in a shipping office as befitted her romantic nature and rented a large grey house on Seymour Street where the Dalhousie University power station now stands. She hired a housekeeper and made extra money by taking in a few boarders – a medical student, a lawyer, a teacher. I became embedded in a neighbourhood gang that congealed around the house next door where my new friend Pete had a pretty sister, a dog named Spot and a brown tent in his back yard.

To octogenarians it's a marvel how long youth lasts and how childhood summers were always sunny. We explored the countryside on bicycles unhindered by much motor traffic. On Friday nights we trooped down Spring Garden Road to the Capitol Theatre on Barrington Street to *The Wizard of Oz, Gone with the Wind* and *For Whom the Bell Tolls* in new Technicolor. On the way home we drank cherry Cokes at the Greek's soda fountain and invaded Pete's kitchen for cold milk and peanut butter-and-marmalade white-bread sandwiches. With a tough little Cape Breton boy named Elmer, who looked and talked like James Cagney, I skipped Friday afternoon civics classes to watch the real James Cagney in gangster films such as *Angels with Dirty Faces*. I delivered newspapers in a neighbourhood that smelt of mildew and poverty and at Christmas worked in the bowels of Simpson's department store, where underpaid, overworked stock boys helped themselves to small presents such as socks and hankies for their families, though only on Christmas Eve.

I became commander, with the rank of major, of the school cadet corps, which with soccer was what I liked best, which seems odd now I have seen too much of the world to be militaristic. My favourite grade nine teacher was Miss Elizabeth Callan, who taught English, a lean, tanned outdoors sort of woman who encouraged my love of books and was one of those teachers with a sense of vocation. I also tried my hand at music with a makeshift drum set and then with a second-hand alto saxophone, learned to read music and joined a teen band – piano, sax, trumpet, clarinet, drums – which stumbled through cheap arrangements of "In the Mood," "The Five O'Clock Whistle," "You Are My Sunshine," "Frenesie" and "Drummer Boy."

Young Major MacKay, age fifteen, commanding a wartime city-wide schools cadet parade two months before tuberculosis ended his school days.

I joined the kilted Boy Scout troop of St. Andrews United Church, having been seduced by the social benefits of religion and lured by the weekends at the Scout cabin at Miller's Lake, a wilderness area before the coming of progress years later in the shape of the Halifax airport. By ferocious cramming in partnership with an older boy we managed to amass enough badges in such disparate and unlikely subjects as map-making, plumbing, woodworking and music to gain the rarified rank of King's Scout so we could join the honour guard attending King George VI and Queen Elizabeth on June 15, 1939. The shy, slender King and his stocky wife arrived in their blue and silver special train after a seven-week trans-Canada publicity tour to inspire Empire solidarity in a world threatened by war. On a perfect Nova Scotia spring day, sunny with a sea breeze, we King's Scouts were on duty at a luncheon attended by Prime Minister Mackenzie King, one of our most effective prime ministers despite being an odd, bland, enigmatic little man. King George looked tired, and ill, so the Queen stood up and thanked us all for "a rare delight" but no one mentioned the imminence of war. In the evening the symbol of the British Empire and his staunch Scottish wife stood waving from the *Empress of Britain* like little king and queen dolls, she in her favourite powder blue, he dressed as Admiral of the Fleet. We hundreds standing on shore down by Point Pleasure Park sang "Will ye no come back agin" and "God Save the King" until the liner disappeared into the murk. Three months later we were at war, twenty-two years after "the war to end all wars."

A fourteen-year-old King's Scout preparing to join an honour guard for King George VI on his visit to Halifax.

Among hundreds of ships seeking refuge at Halifax that autumn was the *Sir James Clark Ross,* a huge Norwegian whaling factory ship with a crew of 300 that had been steaming back from the Antarctic when the Germans invaded Norway. My mother, who often talked of sending me to Royal Roads Naval College in Victoria, met the ship's chief engineer at a party and convinced him to sign me on as an apprentice. The thought of a whale-killing expedition repels me now, but I had no qualms at the time. Having taken to occasionally smoking a pipe that summer, I bought a tin of Prince Albert tobacco, a suitably nautical peaked cap and a blue turtleneck sweater and on Friday afternoon said my farewells at LeMarchant Street School. We were to sail on Monday.

Then disaster. On Sunday afternoon a treacherous uncle-in-law convinced my mother I should stay in school. Monday morning I

The pavilion (far right) where I spent nine months. The Nova Scotia Sanatorium was later demolished to make way for Annapolis Valley Regional Hospital, modern drugs having outdated a sanatorium system that began in the 1890s.

was accordingly back in class, sheepish, disappointed and angry. But I suppose my uncle did me a favour. Had I sailed I might have been at sea far from medical help when I suffered the bloody lung hemorrhage that put me into the sanatorium for my sixteenth birthday.

Instead of going to sea I spent nine months on the airy top floor of a large white wooden pavilion where life slowed to a crawl. Among 400 inmates, mostly invalided soldiers, sailors, airmen and merchant seamen, I was the youngest. Most were as dedicated as I was to getting better as fast as possible and refused to join the feckless few sneaking out at night to play cards in town. The wide windows were open to all weathers, so we looked deceptively rosy-cheeked as we listened on the earphones attached to our beds to soap operas and country and western heartbreak music. Committed to rest, fresh air, wholesome food, I can't recall seeing anyone visibly depressed, but the only good thing I can say about pulmonary tuberculosis is that it causes no physical pain because there are no nerves in the lungs. My pneumothorax treatment was certainly preferable to thoracoplasty, which was surgical removal of ribs. Given its highly infectious nature, fortunately none of my family, friends or schoolmates, so far as I know, caught the disease from me when I was going about for months without knowing I had it.

When my temperature abated and I could get out of bed and stroll around I found a self-contained village: twenty buildings spread over forty acres, a staff of 200, including seven resident doctors, its own electric power, radio station, laboratory, laundry, barber shop, chapel, canteen, school teacher, auditorium, library, post office, magazine and recreation club.

By the time I returned home to Halifax, the city of 60,000 had become one of the most important ports in the western hemisphere, doubled its population and lost its name. For the second time in three decades Halifax was anchoring Britain's lifeline as convoys of

Back home, healthier and several pounds heavier, with friends (left to right) Bob Knight, Fred Meade, Keith Gauvin, Peter Flynn, Bob Walsh and Pete's dog Spot.

merchant vessels glided out of the harbour bound for Britain with food, fuel, troops, guns, ammunition. The garrison Kipling had exalted as "Warden of the Honour of the North" had become an "East Coast Port," a bureaucratic disguise that fooled no one, including the enemy lurking in U-boats off the coast. Crumbling Victorian forts were manned at the mouth of the harbour and a steel anti-submarine net stretched across its mouth between two gate ships and closed at night when submarines had the best chance of slipping through. The war seemed very near the foggy Sunday afternoon we saw a sudden flash out at sea and heard an explosion. The British oil tanker *Kars* carrying 13,000 tons of aviation gasoline had been torpedoed so close to Halifax that we could see her burning for days. Only Tom Black from Scotland survived from a crew of forty. Older citizens that day recalled World War I and the munitions ship explosion which killed 2,000 citizens and wounded 4,000 in the world's worst explosion before that of Hiroshima in 1945.

Nova Scotia having been designated as a "front line area liable to enemy attack," blackouts were introduced and posters warned us that "Loose lips sink ships." Radio stations interrupted programming with strident bars of "Rule Britannia" followed by a mystery voice – "Attention all lighthouse keepers. Instruction A, A for Apple, will be carried out." What precisely the keepers of Nova Scotia's lighthouses were meant to do – turn off the light? change the flashes? – remained a mystery until after the war when we learned that "A-for-Apple" only meant the lights should be kept on.

Bruce Jefferson, a wartime censor and retired newspaperman, described a day in the life of Halifax during the war: "For some time the harbour has been growing noisier at night and the heavy fogs have increased this tendency. Last night was probably the worst since the war began. A convoy of fifty ships was crawling in all night and in addition to the usual loud blowing for the medical boat, pilot launches, coal barges, navigation signals, etc., each vessel blew a fog warning every few yards. It was a still night and to add to the din of customary fog whistles, buoys and bells, each of the ships anchored in the harbour – and there were dozens – maintained an anchor watch who vigorously rang the ship's bell every minute or so. The whole thing was a bedlam which made sleep almost impossible."

Day after day trainloads of uniformed men rolled in from Montreal and Toronto, Winnipeg, Regina, Calgary and Vancouver, to be scooped up by the *Queen Mary, Queen Elizabeth* or the *Empress of Britain* and borne off to England. British naval vessels were often in port and brought otherwise remote stars like Gracie Fields to entertain us colonials in the United Church Hall on Coburg Road.

WALTER S. LEGGETT, LIBRARY AND ARCHIVES CANADA PA-115367

World War II thrust Halifax onto the "front line" and brought an invasion of the military, foreign shipping, air raid sirens, blackouts, rationing and excitement.

Winston Churchill came twice by ship, en route to conferences in Washington and Quebec City.

Everyone seemed bent on patriotism and/or adventure, washed in the propaganda that war was noble and glamorous, and ignoring the part that was desperate, dirty, immoral and deadly. Halifax, being more directly engaged in the war than any other North American city, had for a while become a tourist attraction, especially for Americans, their own nation having so far kept out of it despite Churchill's unceasing efforts to draw them in. I felt out of it too. The misfortune that had denied me normal teen-age years would also rob me of adventure. Or so it seemed, for life can change quickly when one is young.

Completing my recuperation at home and unable and unwilling to return to school after having missed two years, I took comfort from Mark Twain's boast, seconded incidentally by Winston Churchill, that one should never let schooling interfere with education. If education indeed is meant to teach people how to think, a dose of *autodidactos* at least permits the study of subjects one truly wishes to learn rather than subjects dictated by a school board. Having a mother who loved books, I had learned to love them too, not only their contents but their look and smell and feel. By now I was reading Dr. Charles Eliot's "five foot shelf" of Harvard Classics "for young persons whose education had been cut short." To learn how to live as well as for pleasure, I read H.G. Wells, Maugham, Tolstoy, Shaw, Conrad, Hardy, others. In Thomas Mann's *Magic Mountain* I found consolation among the exotic patients at Sanatorium Berghof in Davos.

Having fled the Baptist Church at a tender age, I gravitated to pantheism, to Emerson and Thoreau and the atheistic morality of Spinoza. With my health on the mend I subscribed to mail order courses in history and a particularly useful interactive course in journalism run by moonlighting editors of the *New York Times*. When I was well enough to go to work I got a fresh-air job at a lumber yard at Sheet Harbour east of Halifax. One day I answered an advertisement seeking an editor for a new weekly newspaper in Bridgewater, which was owned by an elderly businessman who knew even less about newspapering than I did. Its sole staff was a surly journeyman linotype operator who had single-handedly been producing the paper and was naturally unimpressed by my inexperience. Thrilled by my first newspaper job, I overreached myself and wrote a column which upset town boosters, including my boss, by questioning the quality of the town's water supply. But fate moved in mysterious ways. When my employer revealed that he had actually hired me to solicit ads, not as a news man, we had a row one Friday afternoon and Saturday morning I departed after less than a month on the job. As I left for Halifax in a car driven by a friendly salesman met at my boarding house, I had a glimpse of my boss speeding toward the railway station before the train left for Halifax. He apparently assumed that because I had arrived by train I was leaving by train. Luckily he failed to spot me or I might have relented and gone back – after all it was my first writing job – and thus missed the lucky opportunity which started my real career.

In Halifax my friend Ted Shields, lame and ineligible for the armed forces, had found editorial work at the Canadian Press news agency. In normal times neither of us would have been considered for the positions of day editor and overnight editor of CP with so little experience. I could type and write English so I was hired for the undemanding overnight hours, which usually meant preparing a few routine local stories for the wire when the teletype operators came to work in the morning, and compressing Canadian news into a money-saving compounded form of wordage called "cablese" for transmission to West Indies newspapers. Ted and I joined the new Halifax Press Club, where, in the days before Halifax pubs, we could smoke and drink beer and dream of becoming foreign correspondents. (We had just seen Joel McCrea in Hitchcock's thrilling 1940 movie of that name.) We bought a fifteen-foot sailboat, which we moored in the Northwest Arm, and took girls cruising on moonlit Saturday nights.

With Ted's departure to university in the fall I was promoted to day editor, which carried somewhat more responsibility and a salary increase to $21 a week, although the backbone of the bureau was always night editor Johnny Leblanc, a lean, laconic middle-aged Acadian who rolled his own cigarettes and taught us the basics of wire service journalism. Without Johnny, bureau manager Andy Merkel would have been in difficulty. A newsman of the old school who had covered the sinking of the *Titanic,* he was in his sixties and on the verge of retirement, stout and florid with a crooked nose and shock of white hair over his forehead. Much of the time I was there he seemed engrossed in his own narrative verses about colonial Nova Scotia, which was fine with me for I could get on with my work more or less free from his occasional temper – former staffers had nicknamed him Grumpy – when things on my trick went wrong.

The worst day of my apprenticeship was the morning after Johnny had worked like a trojan for many overtime hours single-handedly interviewing and writing a dozen separate stories about soldiers – "Canadian heroes" – who had just returned on a hospital ship. He had transmitted half the stories for Canada's morning newspapers and left the other half in a folder on the desk to be transmitted when I came in at 8 a.m. for the afternoon papers. In the rush of the morning I overlooked the folder and by the time I saw it around noon it was too late. I felt ill about the lapse – I still remember it vividly – but when Johnny came in that night he said not a word, which somehow made me feel worse. Apart from Andy Merkel, his pretty secretary, Leblanc and myself the bureau consisted of two veteran teletype operators who sometimes corrected my errors. Without Johnny Leblanc holding the bureau down I would not have lasted the year.

With the war winding down I was restless. I remembered the Norwegian whaler I had been thwarted from joining and my mother's abortive efforts to get me into the naval college in Esquimault. In short, I had sea fever, so I gave in my notice and walked down to the Merchant Marine Manning Pool. I can make no claim that I was keen to "serve my country" or "fight for freedom" or anything like that, for to be honest it was really all about adventure, a response to the Zeitgeist, my wish to be part of something big, to "belong." I'd read about war for years and wanted to see it for myself. I admired Ernest Hemingway in those days for going to World War I as an eighteen-year-old ambulance driver, having been denied military service because of his poor eyesight.

Healthy again and not wanting to miss the war entirely, at the age of nineteen I rounded off a sketchy teenage education by joining the Norwegian merchant marine and going to sea with the blessing of my sea-struck mother and a silver MN merchant navy identity bracelet, a farewell present from a forgiving Andy Merkel.

4

FISKEBOLLER AND FLATBRØD

"The only thing that ever really frightened me during the war was the U-boat peril." Winston Churchill.

On a cold morning in Halifax harbour with snow in the air a cheerful young seaman from Stavanger met me at the gangplank to show me around my new home. The Norwegian oil tanker *Peik* would soon join a convoy bound for Britain.

Our first stop was the crew quarters toward the stern, where even apprentices like me had the luxury of a white-painted, two-bunk cabin rather than the shabby cramped forecastles of older ships. In the gleaming white galley I was offered *"en god kop café"* and promised a constant supply of fresh-baked sugar cookies. Ships' cooks can be bloody-minded, but these two cheerful Norsemen donned white uniforms at five every morning to bake bread and cookies and perform harmonious day-long duets with pots, pans and skillets through rough seas and smooth. Except for bacon and eggs at breakfast, food was Norwegian, bland and white: flatbread, canned fiskeboller made from white fish, white potato balls, cabbage, white semolina puddings laced with caraway and red fruit syrup.

The superstructure at midships housed bridge, chart room, wheelhouse, radio shack and the cabins of Captain Ole Westad Hay and his deck officers. The bow and fore deck were crammed with winches, bollards, anchor chain, hoses and containers of sawdust for sopping up oil spills. Pipes ran the length of the deck, big pipes for loading and smaller pipes for discharging oil from cargo tanks divided into compartments. I'd never seen so many pumps: cargo pumps, ballast

Built in 1930 at Newcastle, England, for a Norwegian company, *Peik* served unscathed throughout World War II, was rebuilt and renamed *Jalna* in 1952, and retired in 1961 to be broken up for scrap at Grimstad.

pumps, lubricating pumps, transfer pumps, sanitary pumps. In the brightly lit white cavern of the engine room, men in greasy blue overalls, wads of cotton wipes overflowing their pockets, would soon be intently watching pistons powerful enough to crush tombstones.

Named for a character in Norse folklore, the M/T (motor tanker) *Peik,* my home for nearly six months, carried a crew of fifty, measured 396 feet by 55 feet, and at 10,000 tons seemed a fair size until I compared her with today's supertankers, which make her seem hardly more than a yacht. Tankers were late-comers to the merchant navy, oil having been shipped in wooden barrels until Ludwig Nobel, Alfred's brother, found a cheaper method of shipping it in 1878. Wooden hulls were leaky so he built steel ships with tanks, which solved the problem of shifting that had sunk earlier attempts, and the booming oil industry spawned fleets of ships. *Peik,* in her wartime role, was an "escort oiler," which meant that in addition to her main occupation of hauling oil from southern U.S. ports to Britain she refuelled her convoy escorts as a sea-going service station. A destroyer or corvette could come alongside and we would send over a hose pipe. Refuelling in an unruly sea while steaming a hundred feet apart could be tricky and messy.

Refuelling a warship at sea in close proximity could be messy, tricky, even dangerous, in other than a calm sea. To start things off, a light line fired from the tanker pulled across a heavier "messenger line" which in turn pulled flexible transfer pipes.

Peik flew the flag of Norway, although she'd not been in her home port of Sandifjord since the Nazis invaded in 1940. Except for two English RNVR gunners, two Canadians and one Australian, the crew were Norwegian and all spoke English. Captain Hay, thin, dark-haired and in his forties, seemed to leave daily details of running the ship to his blond, bustling first officer, whose broken nose belied a kind heart. The chief engineer was a care-worn older man who would pause in whatever he was doing to listen, like a music critic, to the threshing, spinning, thumping steel driving the machinery below.

Having dreamed of going to sea for a long time, I happily settled into a dawn to dark routine of menial labour – swabbing decks, chipping paint, fetching food to the mess – which ashore would have been demeaning and boring. Occasionally, I received instruction in gunnery and such tanker lore as "ullage," monitoring the gap between the surface of the oil and the top of a tank to see whether our volatile cargo was expanding or contracting.

Like most merchant vessels, *Peik* sailed in convoy, a majestic sight as we plugged along toward distant horizons. "Fast" convoys – capable of fifteen knots like *Peik* – left Halifax (HX) every few days and reached Britain in a fortnight, weather permitting. Some made it in ten days. Slower convoys formed up at Sydney, Cape Breton (SC) – and took longer. When convoys were new at the beginning of the war, Convoy HX-1 left Halifax on September 16, 1939, with four escort ships for a fourteen-day journey to Liverpool; its makeup was fairly representative:

Cairneck, general cargo, Newcastle, England

Gloucester City, explosives, London

Hartismere, tobacco, cotton, clay, Liverpool

Consuelo, flour, Hull

Maplewood, wheat, London

Delilian, grain, flour, general cargo, Glasgow

Springdale, pitch and coke, Charente, France

Beaverford, ammunition and general cargo, London

Nova Scotia, general cargo, apples, Liverpool

Henry Desprez, crude oil, Le Havre

Carimare, ballast, Le Havre

Capulet, diesel oil, Liverpool

Vermont, lead and aircraft, Bordeaux

City of Eastbourne, general cargo, Calcutta

Silverlarch, general cargo and oil, Calcutta

Mansepool, general cargo, tobacco, Liverpool.

During the last three months of 1939 there were twenty-two HX convoys made up of 431 ships. All ships except the *Vermont,* which was sunk, arrived unscathed, but in 1940 losses began to mount dramatically.

At any one time there might be half a dozen convoys at sea, perhaps 200 ships hunted by 50 U-boats. The biggest convoy numbered 167 ships spread over 30 square miles. A more typical convoy numbered 35 ships, covering five square miles sailing in nine columns, four or five to a column at intervals of 600 yards. The Commodore, usually a retired naval officer aboard one of the faster cargo ships, marshalled the convoy with flag signals by day and Aldis lamps at night. Before sailing, the master of each ship met with the port Naval Control Officer to get Sailing Orders: "Being in all respects ready for sea, you are to sail in convoy to your destination in accordance with the following instructions.... Your attention is drawn to the urgent necessity of keeping strict accurate stations so as to leave as few tracks as possible." Minesweepers went out to look for submarines and ensure sea approaches were clear; an RCAF plane stayed overhead until the convoy was far offshore.

Early in the war, when Britain had underestimated Hitler's ability to sever her lifeline, U-boats attacked in wolf packs and the toll in ships and vital war supplies was devastating, but by 1944 the wolf pack system had been defeated by better radar and long-range Liberator bombers, which closed the area in mid-ocean where there had been no air protection. Only toward the end of the war, when the Germans were losing, was there a surge in attacks by U-boats equipped with new schnorkel breathing tubes that allowed them to operate continuously under water.

Like the crews of freighters carrying explosives, we received danger pay and were stationed for relative safety in the middle of a convoy. U-boats had been known to sneak into a convoy at night and several of my shipmates had survived "a hammering" on other tank-

The introduction in 1943 of long-range Liberators to guard convoys in mid-ocean, plus the cracking of the German Enigma naval code, were decisive in winning the Battle of the Atlantic by outwitting the dreaded U-boat "Wolf Packs." This photo gives a good view of a convoy spread out across several square miles of ocean.

ers. I can't recall them once mentioning the obvious: that a single acoustic torpedo homing on the sound of *Peik*'s propellers would turn us into a massive torch. Lifeboat drills were frequent and we were warned against showing lights or throwing out rubbish, which attracted U-boats.

When gales turned the Atlantic into ravines and white-topped mountains and *Peik* began plunging and rolling and emitting strange shrieks, I braced myself against the bulkhead to stay in my bunk, grateful I was not aboard Captain Jackie Schmidt's battered little Dutch freighter, half the size of *Peik*. That was to have been my first ship until I noticed that under the bunks in the forecastle several inches of salty water were sloshing around. No one seemed to know where the water was coming from so I was redirected with surprising alacrity to *Peik*, not stopping to consider just why; the Manning Depot was having a hard time finding crews for munitions ships and oil tankers for convoys threatened by a recent resurgence in U-boat activity.

My favourite times were fine evenings when I sat on the stern admiring the seascape with my dinner plate and a cup of coffee and watched ships of the seven seas battening down for the night. Apart from storm or fog, when there was danger of collision with neighbouring vessels, our days oscillated between monotony and alarm. The worst of the U-boat menace was long over, but U-boats were still lurking around to pick off stragglers. They attacked at night and I recall the slow Greek freighter at the tail of our convoy gradually losing power all one afternoon and dropping back until it disappeared in the dusk like a pale ghost. With U-boats nearby the convoy could not wait and in the morning we saw black smoke on the horizon. I learned later that of the more than 200 ships sunk in 377 convoys which left Halifax during the war, at least 60 were said to be stragglers.

Our convoys usually had five escort corvettes of the type Nicholas Monsarratt described in *The Cruel Sea*. Half the length of *Peik*, a corvette was crammed with twice as many men, including youngsters from the landlocked Prairies, which for some reason I never discovered contributed a quarter of Canada's sailors. Such large crews were required to man the mass of equipment and armament on those little ships: 4-inch gun on forecastle, anti-aircraft guns, Hedgehog depth charge launchers, radar to see at night or in fog, Asdic which sent out sounds which returned a pinging echo when they detected a solid object.

The shallow-draft corvette was wet, uncomfortable and bobbed like a cork; the crew were crammed into the forecastle, where there was no privacy and too little sleep. Fresh food could be stored for only four days so there were weeks and weeks of hard tack, corned beef, powdered potatoes and "red lead," which was canned tomatoes. Life was worse on U-boats when the 800-ton VIIC submarines went out on raids two or three months from port with fifty young men living among diesel engines, torpedoes and navigating gear. Apart from tedium and the chance of being discovered and destroyed, living was sordid, with only one toilet and not enough water to wash in. As the German film *Das Boot* relates, after a few days at sea a U-boat was rank with unwashed bodies, sweaty clothes, oil, grease, and food spoiling in high humidity. They breathed fresh air only when they surfaced at night.

Command centres in St. John's, Newfoundland, and Liverpool, England, were like giant board games. When the location of U-boats became known, perhaps through Britain's Enigma code-breaker, naval ratings stuck coloured symbols on wall maps, using red for a ship torpedoed. Meanwhile, out at sea corvettes would be darting about like guard dogs; to be awakened by their whooping sirens was both alarming and comforting as they fired snowflake illumination rockets and dropped depth charges while the convoy zigzagged away. *Peik's* armament consisted of two Oerlikon anti-aircraft guns, sixty depth charges that looked like grey oil drums, and a 12-pounder of World War I vintage mounted on the stern to bluff U-boats into staying submerged. Any U-boat crew who observed our Saturday afternoon practice sessions with that oversized pop gun would have seen shells emerging in a slow, lazy arc to splash harmlessly into the sea, rarely reaching the wooden target we were towing

The only time I saw an enemy submarine up close was in the Irish Sea on May 4, 1945, three days before war's end. At 03:14 a.m. a radio signal from the German naval base at Flensburg had ordered the forty-three U-boats still at sea to surface and fly a black flag of surrender. Eight hours later I was on deck when one of those U-boats surfaced, menacing, black and dripping. We had no idea of its intentions, but knew the frigate HMCS *Strathadam* had only recently been destroyed by U-1302 in these same waters and had heard of U-boat captains vowing to fight on. So there was trepidation as well as curiosity until dishevelled Germans began popping up through the conning tower. The elite of the German navy were unshaven, pale and grubby and my impression was how young they looked. Their captain was twenty-seven. It was easy at that moment to forget that these were people we'd feared and hated and I wanted to ask them if being cooped up in iron coffins for months had been worth it. Given Nazi censorship I doubted they were aware Germany had lost 783 U-boats and 37,000 of their U-boat service comrades killed or captured. For the Allies, estimates vary widely but it is believed the price was well over 2,700 Allied merchant ships sunk and over 70,000 seamen killed. The Norwegians, among whom I served, lost 576 ships and 3,734 sailors.

*   *   *

Hitler was dead, the Third Reich in ruins, the war at an end. In fine weather we sailed north to Scotland where Canadian warships were herding fifteen U-boats in from the Atlantic for a mass surrender ceremony. From Loch Ewe, long and narrow amid barren hills, lonely white cottages, flocks of sheep and subtropical gardens warmed by the Gulf Stream, we sailed alone without escorts around Cape Wrath to Scapa Flow in the Orkneys, base of the British Home Fleet. Although a natural harbour supposedly immune from attack, it was there at high tide on the night of October 14, 1939, that U-47 had sneaked in and torpedoed a thirty-foot hole in the battleship *Royal Oak* with the loss of 800 British sailors.

At Scapa Flow we toasted VE-Day with weak beer or lemon squash and danced with jolly Scots and English girls of the Women's Royal

A rare view of a surfacing Nazi U-boat. The only time the *Peik* encountered one so close was at the end of the war when a U-boat unexpectedly surfaced to surrender.

Naval Service in an ugly prefabricated hall. Outside, the northern sun shone on treeless fields until well after midnight, ensuring there was nowhere for amorous couples to settle; our purser had dutifully distributed condoms to the crew to no purpose. From Scapa Flow we sailed alone down the North Sea to the Firth of Forth, in an area where a German submarine, U-2336, had just ignored the ceasefire and torpedoed the Canadian freighter *Avondale Park* with the loss of two lives, the last Allied ship sunk in World War II.

After a brief spell at Rosyth dockyard we sailed with the destroyers HMS *Valorous* and *Venomous* across the North Sea into the Skagerrak and the port of Kristiansand, south of Oslo. It had been one of Germany's last U-boat bases, captured recently by the British, and we were the first free Norwegian vessel to sail up the fiord, our flags flying, our loud speakers blaring *"Eisken dette Landet,"* the Norwegian national anthem. We were entertained to an all-day victory party. I'd heard that the Nobel Prize-winning author Knut Hamsun, then in his eighties, was living in a retirement home in Grimstad and I mentioned how much I admired his novel *Growth of the Soil.* My hosts, members of the underground resistance, said Hamsun had been a Nazi sympathizer and refused to help me arrange a visit to him, which perhaps was just as well for I've since discovered it is rarely a good idea to meet an author you admire.

From Norway we sailed down the Kattegat to Copenhagen, which was then being cleansed of the long German occupation. Our usual fate was to dock at a tank farm far from a town, so we were pleased to lie in downtown Copenhagen, where gun-toting civilians with the arm bands of freedom fighters had taken over from Germans guarding the docks. They greeted our Norwegian crew like brothers and, carrying rifles, revolvers and tommy guns, escorted us on a pub crawl that began on the waterfront at Langelinie and straggled on to Tivoli Gardens with its restaurants and fun fair. While we were there shots were heard and we were told that the hated HIPOS (*Hilfepolizei*), an auxiliary police force of Nazi sympathizers, were sniping from the wooded outskirts of the fifteen-acre pleasure grounds.

Copenhagen had suffered little damage, for the Nazis had been careful to preserve Denmark's agricultural economy for their own ends. After the austerities of Britain and Norway I found an abundance of food and drink and unrationed consumer goods although tobacco was scarce. With our new friends, the freedom fighters, the nights were a continual party in which they insisted on plying us with beer and aquavit. Late one night walking back to my ship and having had too much to drink, I sat on a bench to rest and became aware of an apparition in white standing over me. In the street light she was pretty and young and fragrant. I knew enough Norwegian to understand *"Hvor kommer du fra?"* so was able to reply that I came from Canada. She asked, *"Taler du engelsk?"* And when I assured her I did, she too spoke English, like so many Scandinavians. When she invited me "to her place," I agreed without stopping to wonder what a nice young woman was doing walking the streets at 2 a.m. I strolled along with her for two blocks until half a dozen British paratroopers loomed out of the dark and pre-empted her attention. She had seemed so nice I regretted her change of plans but found my way, unrequited, back to my ship to wake up for work at 7 a.m. with a pounding hangover.

From Copenhagen we sailed to Germany and bombed-out Bremerhaven. The streets were rubble, buildings empty roofless shells, the citizens dazed and fearful and British troops were hunting down "werewolves," armed young diehard Nazis. I saw many German soldiers, men who had fought the Russians, looking hungry and tired and begging for cigarettes. While I was there the British arrested a vagrant, who turned out to be Heinrich Himmler, who committed suicide rather than face a war crimes court.

Peik's voyage back to the United States took us through the English Channel, which had been closed to shipping most of the war. Although I'd experienced rougher weather in mid-Atlantic, to my embarrassment I suffered my first and only seasick attack, surprised at its virulence. For a night and a day I lay in my bunk, immobile and uncaring whether I lived or died. By the time we put into an English port for supplies I woke up to find my treacherous Canadian cabin mate had deserted ship with all his belongings and my Nazi mementoes, a Luger pistol and an ornate SS ceremonial dagger I had traded cigarettes for in Bremerhaven.

The week spent crossing the Atlantic to the United States with everyone relaxed and cheerful was like a sunny summer cruise. For the first time *Peik* showed her running lights. In Baltimore the wait for my pay in a stifling dockyard was bearable because I explored nightlife with an attractive Blackfoot Indian girl from Arizona. She was a wartime dockyard riveter but you'd never think so to see her dolled up and out on the town.

As for *Peik,* she was sold and renamed *Jalna,* like the town in the

novels of Canadian Mazo de la Roche. I have failed to find out why a
Norwegian ship was named after a fictional Canadian town. In 1961
Peik/Jalna was broken up for scrap at Grimstad. There are no ships
like her now and the merchant navy is a different world. Tankers are
automated and computer experts and technicians rank with skip-
pers and chief engineers. *Peik* and her like were nearly the last of the
traditional merchant vessels before the era of super-ships which look
like floating warehouses.

My journey was not yet over. Having worked for the Canadian
Press in Halifax, on my way home by train I visited CP's New York
office, and there amid teletypes and ticker tape I had one of those
encounters that change one's life. I was introduced to the newest CP
trainee or "copy girl," Margaret Anderson from the northern logging
town of Cochrane, Ontario, who had quit her English courses at the
University of Toronto to live with her Aunt Hazel in Manhattan.
Flush with danger pay, I invited her to dinner and a Broadway play,
The Dark of the Moon. For the next four evenings we met in bars or the
Greenwich Village flats of her friends; because I had just come from

sea I was an oddity among
these pale, hard-drinking
Canadian expatriates. An attractive, dark-haired Nova
Scotia clergyman's daughter
named Jackie looked into my
eyes and asked, "But who *are*
you?" A few years later she

Margaret Annetta Anderson,
twenty, from Cochrane, Ontario,
when an apprentice journalist at
the Canadian Press office in New
York, summer 1945.

was the inspiration for the self-destructive young Peggy Sanderson in Morley Callaghan's Montreal novel *The Loved and the Lost*. Unlike Peggy, however, she did not end up raped and murdered, but after a life in which she went to sea on a Norwegian ship and fell in love with the first mate, whom she married and divorced, she lived in northern Norway by herself until her death in her late seventies.

Margaret and I talked of books and plays and consumed excessive quantities of hard liquor, as people did in those days, and explored cellar joints in the brownstones of Swing Alley on 52nd Street, where for the price of a couple of beers you could hear the best jazz in the world. Margaret loved late nights though she had to be at work early each morning, whereas I could sleep to noon in my room in the Emerson Hotel, but she was always game for another night out on the town. On the fourth night we parted with friendly kisses and I took the train next morning for Nova Scotia.

Homecoming began as anticlimax. My mother had not received my telegram and was visiting friends. Halifax, exhausted by the war, was recovering from the riot and looting that had made the city infamous on VE-Day, and while I was trying to climb through the back window of my mother's Queen Street apartment a policeman arrived. I convinced him I was no burglar. I was in the kitchen brewing coffee when it suddenly seemed that Halifax was suffering a rerun of the war. Hearing what sounded like distant fireworks, I turned on the radio and heard that the Bedford Basin naval ammunition dump, overloaded with shells and depth charges, was on fire. As darkness fell, a towering red flame appeared over the north end of the city and a reporter spoke of an ominous mushroom cloud and thoughts turned to the disastrous explosion of World War I. People were evacuated from northern neighbourhoods but despite heavy property damage there was amazingly only one fatality.

5

THE UNKNOWN COUNTRY

Early in World War II two books appeared with the message that
Canada was burdened with an identity problem.

Describing Canada in the cadences of Shakespeare's *Richard II,*
Hugh MacLennan's Halifax novel *Barometer Rising* spoke of "This
unborn mightiness, this question mark ... undiscovered by the rest
of the world and unknown to itself, neither American nor English."
At the same time, in *The Unknown Country: Canada and Her People,* British Columbia journalist Bruce Hutchison claimed in a book
written for Americans that "Canada is, among the important nations of the world, the least known." Lyrically describing vast spaces,
forests, lakes and lonely prairies framing the fringe of settlement
hugging the U.S. border, he wrote, "My country has not found itself
nor felt its power nor learned its true place."

Although MacLennan and Hutchison had been describing the
pre-war Canada of the 1930s and earlier and the country was changing rapidly, the fact remained that seventy years after Confederation,
and ten since the Statute of Westminster had made Canada an equal
partner in the British Commonwealth, our national flag was still the
United Kingdom's Union Jack, our national anthem "God Save the
King" and our passports identified us as "British subjects."

As the postwar Empire crumbled, Canada shrugged off enough
colonialism to emerge as one of the few nations intact and growing. A new Citizenship Act ensured that "British subjects" would
henceforth be "Canadian citizens." At the time they were mostly of
French, English, Scottish, Irish, German, Scandinavian, Ukrainian,
Jewish, Dutch, Polish Italian, Chinese, Japanese and First Nation

ancestry. As migration from Britain and Ireland waned, the government sought more Poles, Ukrainians, Germans, Austrians and Dutch.

During the next five years I was fortunate to have work which took me across the country to explore Canada's identity for myself. In September 1945 I was hired by British United Press (BUP), Canadian affiliate of the New York-based news agency United Press, which had a reputation of offering young recruits rapid promotion and international travel to compensate for low wages. For the first eighteen months my beat was the Maritimes, which Hutchison called a "run-down" source of emigration, though there had been a piping time when its tall ships had conquered the mercantile world from Hong Kong to Stockholm. Andrew Merkel summed up those years in one of his ballads: "In Eighteen Sixty-four ... Plenty strode long limbed about the land ... The Golden Brand of Nova Scotia tugged and felt the breeze. From myriad masts in all the seven seas." That free and easy time had vanished with Confederation and iron steamships. Although Maritimers knew how to fashion wooden sailing ships and possessed the iron and coal to build and run steamships, they had inexplicably failed to compete in the age of steam. Now in the postwar 1940s prosperity was returning, fuelled by exports of farm produce, wood and fish and the demand for homes, schools, hospitals, factories, consumer goods and popular culture.

Our news output in this quiet corner of the world was mostly about the aftermath of war and return to peacetime pursuits, and an irregular mixture of politics, coal mine accidents and air and sea disasters. When "hard news," which is to say the unexpected or unusual, was lacking there were annual rehashes of regional features such as the Oak Island treasure pit in Mahone Bay, inspired by the 1849 gold rush on the Pacific Coast. Oak Island was the hiding place of Captain Kidd's treasure until someone inconveniently remembered his treasure had been found in New Jersey and produced at his 1701 trial in

There was glamour in news work. Young reporters accepted meagre wages because of assurances of early promotion and the chance to work abroad in an organization with so many clients in so many time zones that the United Press motto was "a deadline every minute."

London. The notion that someone from somewhere had done something mysterious on the island kept people doggedly digging, despite great expense and occasional loss of life, deaf to rational evidence their treasure pit was a sink hole which the sea kept flooding with odd effects. It was Nova Scotia's Loch Ness Monster.

Stories more creditable came from the growing number of postwar immigrants such as Ann Johnson, who had been a nursing sister in a hospital in Renfrewshire, Scotland, when one night in 1941 she was called out in an ambulance and found a farmer with a pitchfork standing over an injured pilot. The pilot was Hitler's lieutenant Rudolf Hess, who had flown to Britain in his abortive effort to talk the British aristocracy into ending the war, which resulted in Hess becoming a prisoner.

Another war prisoner was the subject of one my few stories to make the *New York Times*, whose moonlighting editors had taught me journalism by mail while I was convalescing from TB. Someone discovered that one of Hitler's early henchmen was living in Paradise, a hamlet amid the apple blossoms of the Annapolis Valley. We'd heard that Nazis were sneaking into Canada but none so close to Hitler as Otto Strasser. The British government had brought Strasser to Canada in 1941 to organize a "Free German" movement in North America. Stocky, middle-aged, intense and wearing a European beret, Strasser was not averse to publicity for reasons I was slow to appreciate because I knew nothing of his importance to the early Nazi movement, or how he and his brother Gregor had quarrelled with Hitler, who rejected their socialist views. When Hitler had Gregor murdered, Otto fled with a price on his head and published *Hitler and I*, which warned that *der Fuehrer* was a psychopath who "pulls down the walls without any idea of what he will build in their place...." Now Strasser was living above a country shop and complaining he was denied travel papers to return to Germany to expound socialist neo-Nazism. Ten years later when I was living in Munich I heard that he had finally been allowed to return and had started a political party; he died in the 1970s having made little impact in a Germany which wanted to forget the war.

The dark side of rural Nova Scotia was revealed in the sad case of the Butterbox Babies. Premonitions of tragedy had appeared in 1936 when William and Lila Young, a chiropractor and midwife who ran the "Ideal Maternity Home and Sanatarium" near the prosperous yachting town of Chester, were charged with manslaughter. They were acquitted by a jury although a mother and her newborn baby had died while in their care, allegedly due to negligence and dirt.

In the following years more infant deaths than normal occurred at their Ideal Maternity Home, but despite sinister rumours the Youngs were permitted to operate their facility for unmarried mothers ten more years. Eventually the two were convicted, not of manslaughter but of illegally selling black-market babies to the United States, for which they were fined and driven out of business. The worst was to come. After their baby farm had been shut down and they'd fled to Quebec, bodies of unmarketable babies – malformed, malnourished, ill – were found in little pine boxes and mass graves.

We transmitted our stories by teletypes which, like the brass telegraph key invented in the 19th century, are so antiquated now I feel obliged to give an idea how they worked. When there was time, we wrote our report on a manual typewriter and then retyped it on a clattering teletype machine that punched holes in a paper tape that corresponded to letters of the alphabet. The tape was fed through a transmitting device at sixty words a minute or more to send the text to other teletype machines. Sometimes for speed we composed directly "on line," typing hot news right into the communications system.

Apart from making a living, my main concern was education. Working the night shift I was able during the day to attend university at a time when many of my fellow students were war veterans. I took courses in history, political science and literature at King's College and Dalhousie University before there was a journalism school. I had been dropping into the waterfront Merchant Seamen's Club for a beer and the foreign papers, and when the manager's apartment in the basement fell vacant I acquired it at a low rent. Though not involved in campus life, I met girls and went to parties but the young woman I had wined and dined in Manhattan that summer began invading my dreams.

Margaret Anderson was attractive, adventurous, fun, a book lover, a freer spirit than any other girl I'd ever met. On impulse one day I sent her a telegram and Margaret and I began a lively correspondence, long-distance phone calls being rare and expensive. She had been living with an aunt, who was concerned that Margaret, barely twenty at the time, was too addicted to Manhattan night life and needed a change of scene. A few months later she joined me in Halifax and became a reporter on the Halifax *Chronicle*, which was a step up from her CP apprenticeship in NY. Margaret arrived by train from New York on a January Friday night in a snowstorm so thick the foghorn was moaning in the harbour and I had to hire a horse and sleigh to fetch her trunk from the station.

We celebrated with a dinner at the Nova Scotian Hotel, then virtually the only good dining room in the city. For $500 I bought an old sailboat, which we christened *Peik* and moored on the Northwest Arm. She was a twenty-five-foot sloop-rigged keel boat with mainsail and jib, a small cabin but no motor, which meant she was not equipped for coastal cruising. We went cruising anyway and created a crisis: One afternoon, the wind light, the sun warm, Margaret and I and our friends Pete Flynn, who was studying engineering, and Harry Rhude, a wartime fighter pilot studying law, set off on a cruise that was supposed to take us along the granite coast and get us to the shelter of St. Margaret's Bay by nightfall.

On a similar summer's day fifty years earlier, Captain Joshua Slocum in his motorless sloop *Spray* had sailed this same shore to commence his single-handed, 46,000-mile, three-year voyage around the world. According to his log for July 3, 1895, at 6:45 p.m. he was, like us, off Sambro Light and "the Rock of Lamentations and at 9 p.m. fog lowered over the sea like a pall ... a world of fog shut off from the universe." Single-handed ocean crossings have become common in our 21st century world of navigational aids, radio and ubiquitous rescue organisations, but in 1895 Slocum was the true pioneer with neither motive power, radio, sponsor or insurance. We in little *Peik* also had none of those amenities but of course we were only going to St. Margaret's Bay. We'd sailed out of Halifax past Herring Cove, Portuguese Cove and Ketch Harbour, our speed equal to a leisurely stroll on land. After we passed Sambro Light the weather deteriorated, as it had for Slocum, and having no motor we were obliged to tack into a stiff headwind with waves breaking over the bow.

The old green rowboat we'd been towing as a tender all day began

to flip over in the swell so
we weighted its stern with
our anchor, the only heavy
thing we had, remem-
bering to rope it to the
mast of the yacht. While
we were doing that Pete
fell off the slippery stern
and disappeared into our
wake. He was not wearing
a life jacket and without
the manoeuvrability of a
motor to turn us around
his life was in danger. The
sea was rough and cold
and we feared momentar-
ily we'd lost him but he
grabbed the edge of the
deck and clung with his
fingernails, only his face showing. Luckily, he was wearing a sweater

The MacKays preparing for the ill-fated
cruise down the rock-bound Nova Scotia
coast on the yacht *Peik*, towed here by
friend Pete Flynn in the recalcitrant $12
dinghy that saved our lives.

with a thick collar. I, being at the tiller and closest to him, managed
to reach back and hang on to his collar until we could all haul him
in, heavy and dripping.

It was dark and foggy off Shad Bay when we spotted a flashing
light and agreed it was the signal to direct us around the rocks off
Peggy's Cove and into St. Margarets Bay. We were mistaken. With a
strong wind pushing behind us the place we turned into was not the
wide and welcoming St. Margaret's Bay but a strange rocky inlet, too
narrow to come about in under sail and we were now going very fast.
Ahead white water was breaking over rocks.

If there are guardian angels ours was a cranky twelve-dollar rowboat. Having behaved itself for a while, for no apparent reason it

suddenly turned turtle and threw out the anchor, which fortunately caught and brought *Peik* up short, our bow pointing into the wind with sails flapping. We were saved. Fog was coming on thick as we blew hopefully on our little tin fog horn. Within twenty minutes a long slender boat sped silently out of the fog, propelled by six rowers, who towed *Peik* safely to the fishing village of East Dover, which in those days was not reached by road. The fishermen and their wives gave us hot soup and blankets in the schoolhouse and in the morning, after paying $100 for the net we ripped when we accidentally anchored, we sailed through lifting fog into St. Margaret's Bay.

That autumn BUP assigned me to holiday relief in Toronto, which was beginning to challenge Montreal as the economic powerhouse of manufacturing and mining. Despite the incursion of cultural Americanization, Toronto had clung to British traditions and Presbyterian morality, so it was ironic that in "Toronto the good" I received my first (and surprisingly last) bribe in my thirty-year career as a journalist. Seventeen years before Canada decided on its distinctive red and white national flag with the maple leaf, I'd had a phone call from a Quebec Member of Parliament visiting Toronto to publicize his design for a Canadian flag. I met him in his room at the King Edward Hotel, where he offered me a glass of Scotch and soda and a cigar. His design was not unattractive – I forget if it was a beaver, maple leaf or a cross – and I told him I intended to write a brief item. As I was leaving and shaking hands he left a piece of paper in my hand as he closed the door. It was a five dollar bill, a fourth of my weekly salary. I learned later that was a common courtesy among Quebec politicians.

In Halifax that fall Margaret and I discovered we did not want to be parted again. The casual custom of simply living together being still in the future, we decided to marry, although Margaret's strict church-going parents in Toronto warned her she was too young. Being twenty-one and self-supporting, on the last night of 1946 we were married in the chapel of King's College by one of my two history professors, who was an Anglican clergyman. Neither Margaret nor I was religious but the candlelight service, in which a Merchant Navy friend, Howard Greer, who was studying to be an Anglican priest, unexpectedly sang the liturgical responses, was moving to both of us. No one owned a car then so our wedding party of twelve rode noisily home through the dark, icy streets in a clanking yellow streetcar to drink black rum and Coke in our flat in the Seamen's Club. I was happy. Margaret had completed something, banished loneliness, opened horizons which had nothing to do with the images of a suburban home, parent-teacher meetings or commuting. We were twenty-one with our sights set on Europe.

In 1948 I was transferred to Montreal. My successor in Halifax was blond, twenty-year-old Knowlton Nash, who arrived on the train from Toronto with a big suitcase and a straw hat, which I had never seen on a young man before but only on the elderly. Knowlton was beginning an ambitious career that took him to the anchor chair of the CBC-TV newscast The National.

As for myself, like many Maritimers, I was "going down the road," which for an earlier generation, including my mother and an uncle, had meant work in "the Boston States" but for me meant Montreal.

6

MONTREAL AND WINNIPEG

Montreal in 1947 looked foreign. In the years before high-rise office blocks, subway trains and underground malls, it was a North American city unlike any other. For us from elsewhere, the stone-built metropolis dominated by Church and Mammon mingled the nighttime excitement of Manhattan with the daytime glamour of Paris.

During a fresh fall of snow Old Montreal was a fairy-tale city. Black-clad priests and nuns hurried through streets whose spires, pealing bells and cobblestones recalled northern France. But in one of the largest francophone cities in the world, where the language of swearing – *baptême! tabernac!* – came from the liturgy, the language of commerce remained the tongue of conquerors and carpetbaggers. Bilingualism was the burden of the francophone majority, for whom St. Lawrence Boulevard, "the Main" (Saint-Laurent du Main), was an invisible frontier – French to the east, English to the west, and between them a ghetto of mean streets redolent with the accents and foods of Mittel Europa.

Just west of the Main, Margaret and I found a small apartment in an old house on the fringe of the fading neighbourhood called the Square Mile, once the richest residential address in all of Canada. Long before the invention of income tax, the bearded Scottish merchants who pioneered Canadian industry and commerce lived there on the southern flank of Mount Royal in monumental Palladian and neo-Gothic homes. Prime examples were George Stephen and his cousin Donald Smith, who made fortunes in finance, railways, dry goods and flour mills and died as Lord Mount Stephen and Lord

Strathcona. Richard Angus of the Bank of Montreal waxed rich with coal, iron and steel, pulp and paper; Hugh Allan from Glasgow founded a transatlantic steamship line and lived in Ravenscrag, later a mental institution, which looms like Dracula's Castle over the Square Mile from Mount Royal. Their successors were Edwardian capitalists and financiers such as the Dublin-born civil engineer Herbert Holt, who was accustomed to construction camps before he moved into a house on Stanley Street with fourteen bedrooms, seven bathrooms, and a floor-to-ceiling fireplace decorated with the family crest.

One of the first French Canadians in that charmed Anglophone circle was Quebec-born Rodolphe Forget, who built his yellow brick mansion in Gallic Beaux Arts style. Alfred Baumgarten, the German-born sugar miller, built his house like a Black Forest hunting lodge. One of the last of the old-style tycoons, John W. McConnell, was a boy from Ulster farming stock who left school in Ontario at fourteen, ran errands in Toronto and began his business career at age twenty-three selling bonds in Montreal. A handsome, charming promoter, he became one of the richest men in Canada with interests in mining, public transit, sugar milling, insurance, directorships in two dozen companies and ownership of the city's biggest newspaper, the *Montreal Star*.

At the height of their power fifty Square Mile families controlled much of Canada's commerce and adorned their limestone office buildings on St. James Street with family crests and busts of Mercury, god of business. They imported English servants, gave discreet lawn parties, sent their daughters to finishing schools, and rode to hounds at the Hunt Club, which met in the fields behind Mount Royal every autumnal weekend. Stephen Leacock, who lived among them when he taught economics at McGill University, called the Square Mile "Plutoria-under-the elms." The mansions and their owners, which I was to commemorate later in *The Square Mile: Merchant Princes of Montreal* published in 1987, were already disappear-

Ravenscrag, built by shipping magnate Sir Hugh Allan, became the Allan Memorial Institute in 1943 where Dr. Ewen Cameron performed experiments with LSD and eletroconvulsion on unsuspecting psychiatric patients on behalf of the CIA's MKUltra Project.

ing, as the elms would too when Dutch elm disease arrived. The best of times, I was told, were the Edwardian years before World War I demolished the old conventions and people moved on to neighbouring modern Westmount.

Montreal with a million people became a metropolis not by size or wealth alone but "by consent, tradition, history, and sheer character," wrote Bruce Hutchison in *The Unknown Country*, adding that there was "a touch of wickedness, for beneath all the culture, the refinement and luxury is not only poverty but an organized underworld of vice and crime." Quebec's liquor laws encouraged a proliferation of bars, night clubs, gambling hells, restaurants and "watering holes" such as our alternative "press club" at the memorably named Slitkin's and Slotkin's, aka boxing promoters Lou Wyman and Jack Rogers, which attracted sportsmen as well as reporters.

During the glory years which began with Prohibition, Americans came by the trainload to be greeted by hostesses like Texas Guinan of the Frolics Cabaret on the Main, whose greeting was a cheery "Hello, suckers!" At the Café Saint Michel on Mountain Street, trumpeter Louis Metcalf led a cosmopolitan band which featured a Japanese-Canadian trombonist, Butch Watanabe, and clarinetist Yardbird Benny Weinstein from Glasgow. The Faisan Doré on the Main had known Charles Aznavour, the Sans Souci had heard Édith Piaf in person. Chez Maurice Danceland on St. Catherine Street brought in Tommy Dorsey, Glenn Miller and Cab Calloway. At the Alberta Lounge tall, handsome young Oscar Peterson, the sleeping car porter's son now recovered from the TB which caused him to give up the trumpet, played barrelhouse boogie-woogie. At the Gayety Theatre lissome Marie Klarquist from Minneapolis, the Swede better known as Lili St. Cyr, Queen of the Strippers, entranced us with her erotic ballet danced to classical music. Romantic Lili, who survived six marriages and as many lovers, performed her sensual magic across America but said she loved Montreal best.

To the best of my memory, I never heard the incendiary word "separatism" but a quickening Quebec nationalism had shown itself in the livelier French literature of Jean-Charles Harvey, Gabrielle Roy and Marie-Claire Blais. An avant garde of artists calling themselves *Automatistes* became influential, led by the painter Paul-Émile Borduas, who campaigned for the separation of church and state. Along with Théatre du Rideau Vert, they defied the repressive Premier Maurice Duplessis and puritanical Jansenist bishops. At the same time young Irving Layton and Louis Dudek were creating fresh-sounding Anglophone poetry which was being kept alive by John Sutherland's magazine *First Statement,* which he in turn kept alive by working as a milkman. Mavis Gallant, an attractive, dark-haired young reporter then working for McConnell's weekly *Standard,* had already seen her short stories make the *New Yorker* and was dreaming of Paris, as was teen-aged Mordecai Richler from St. Urbain Street. Down at the Montreal *Gazette* Brian Moore from Belfast was hon-

Called "Harlem of the North" for its jazz joints, Montreal boasted over forty places of entertainment such as Shiller's "Harlem Nites" and Rockhead's Paradise, owned by Jamaican-born Rufus Rockhead, where Billie Holliday, Ella Fitzgerald, Oscar Peterson, Louis Armstrong and Pearl Bailey were known to drop in.

ing skills that would serve him as the author of *The Luck of Ginger Coffey* and so many other successful novels.

The late 1940s was a lively news time dominated by the new Cold War, the phrase coined by George Orwell during World War II and given currency by American presidential advisor Bernard Baruch in a speech in 1947. In Canada Igor Gouzenko, a Russian cypher clerk, had done his bit by setting off a decade of witch hunts when he fled the Soviet embassy in Ottawa with evidence a Red spy ring had penetrated the good grey Canadian government. As in the United States, where Senator Joe McCarthy was soon to launch his infamous rabble-rousing attacks on human rights, Canada was infected with the fears that produced symptoms of the very tyranny we were supposed to be fighting. The treatment of Polish-born Communist MP Fred Rose of Montreal, sentenced to nearly five years in prison and deprived of Canadian citizenship though pleading innocent of espionage, detonated an intense civil liberties debate on how suspects were held, questioned and convicted.

British United Press in McConnell's Montreal Star building on St. James Street was not a typical Canadian newsroom, for among my colleagues were a lord, a count, an award-winning novelist, a defrocked Irish Jesuit and several newly-immigrant Britons. Typically of the time, there was a token woman reporter but no francophones except for the translators working on our French-language service. Our general manager, multilingual, silver-haired Count Robert W. Keyserlingk, was Hollywood's idea of a European diplomat. The son of Count Henry Keyserlingk, who had been a commander in the Russian Imperial Navy, Bob Keyserlingk had escaped the revolution via Japan and Vancouver, where he attended the University of British Columbia. He was a compelling salesman, adept at taking advantage of gaps in the services of our bigger, older rival, Canadian Press, such as creating a lucrative new radio news wire in the 1930s for announcers, untrained in news, in the burgeoning commercial radio station market.

Herbert Sallans, a former editor-in-chief of the *Vancouver Sun,* British Columbia's biggest daily, was my boss on the news side. Tall, thin and tentative amid the noisy teletypes, Herb had won the Governor General's Award for his novel *Little Man.* There was Lord William Shaughnessy, our extrovert young bureau manager, who grew up in the Square Mile and was called Shag by his friends and Bill by us. Grandson of the third president of the Canadian Pacific Railway, Bill had been a wartime major in the Grenadier Guards and was soon to depart for London to occupy his seat in the House of Lords.

Shortly after I arrived in Montreal, New York-based United Press began Americanizing its Canadian franchise, making it more like UP in the States. A smiling salesman-type from California, blond, plump Phil Curran, became our general manager and the exotic Bob Keyserlingk departed to found *The Ensign,* a conservative Catholic journal notable for his obsessive campaign against Communism. Phil Curran, incidentally, was the first person I'd ever seen with the automatic professional smile, peculiar to California businessmen and politicians, which comes and goes like a tic, a neon sign which sheds no warmth. Phil's lieutenant Denny Landry didn't smile at all, a tough little old-time newsman from Boston, who was perpetually concerned with whether we were "cutting the mustard" and gave CP serious competition.

Margaret and I had been in Montreal for a year in 1948 when Phil invited us to dine at Drury's on Dominion Square, a lovely sixty-year-old London-style chop house where famous visitors were treated to the best steaks and chops in the city. Phil had decided to send me to Winnipeg to manage a news region stretching from the Ontario border to the Rockies, with bureaus in Regina, Calgary and Edmonton. Travelling on a CN sleeper, we arrived in Winnipeg while there was spring slush on the wide, windy streets and cops were just doffing their buffalo-hide overcoats. Spread out on the empty prairie, Winnipeg's only faint similarity to Montreal was Wellington Crescent, where the grain barons had built mansions, mock Tudor as it happened, the largest being famous for its thirty-seven rooms, nine fireplaces and seven bathrooms and for being, briefly, the abode of the Prince of Wales. Margaret found us an attic apartment high among trees at the confluence of the Red and Assiniboine rivers, where she painted the walls white and the wooden floors a cheerful yellow. We missed Montreal food – Dunn's, where a twelve-ounce charcoal broiled rib steak cost $1.50, or Ben's Delicatessen, which was open all night to dispense smoked meat sandwiches – but enjoyed our first genuine Chinese cooking, as opposed to chop suey, which we found in a steamy backroom attached to a laundry.

My first task was western coverage of the 1949 general election, in which the avuncular Louis St. Laurent, who had succeeded wily Liberal leader Mackenzie King, easily defeated the Conservatives. Electioneering was less stressful in those days. Party leaders travelling by leisurely train made a dozen key speeches promising different goodies to different regions but communications were so sketchy that lies told in one region never became known in another.

BUP occupied a rented a cut-rate windowless office in the old McIntyre Block near the corner of Portage and Main, where we sweltered in the hot prairie summer. One of my predecessors, perhaps the same penny-pincher who had rented the office, had had the poor idea of paying a good part of the rent by letting two sporting gentlemen sneak peeks at our racing track wire from the States. This allowed obviously illegal bookies to learn race results faster than anyone else, with obvious advantages. Disentangling us from the bookies called for diplomacy, since it meant both BUP and our shady friends lost money.

We maintained a ten-person bureau in Winnipeg and one-person offices in Regina, Calgary and Edmonton. My job was to oversee regional news-gathering and otherwise liaise with client newspapers and radio stations, which meant I travelled to Moose Jaw, Red Deer and Banff on CPR steam trains in cosy, mahogany sleeping cars and elegant dining cars with sealed windows, air conditioning and four-course meals, linen tablecloths and crested silver and china. The prairie provinces – close to a thousand miles of lakes, rivers, sloughs, forests, hills, badlands – surprised me with their variety, and the wind-driven waves across the wheat reminded me of the ocean. In the land of the big sky every few miles there was a red grain elevator, a few houses, a Chinese restaurant, a pool hall. Winnipeg, like Halifax, was not exactly a major world news centre. There was not even

Margaret laden with groceries on an improvised wooden walkway to our front door as the Red River creeps up around the house . On May 5, Black Friday, many residents of the city were evacuated.

much serious crime, as was evident the day the city police blotter led off with the complaint that a reporter who had been writing about city pickpockets had had one of his articles picked from his pocket. It was one of the few Winnipeg stories that made *Time* magazine that year. But I did get to cover one big international story.

Although I'd heard that Winnipeg's name in Cree means "murky water," I had no reason to expect I would soon be covering the most catastrophic flood ever seen in Canada. After a rainy autumn and snowy winter, in April 1950 the Red River, flowing north from Minnesota, turned farmland between the border and Winnipeg into an inland sea. Spring rains filled the river higher hour by hour, flooding streets and homes. Five thousand soldiers were brought in to man pumps, fortify dikes with sand bags and evacuate residents in the biggest peacetime military operation in Canadian history. One sunny afternoon I went to Winnipeg airport and hitched a ride on a small private plane. The Red River had become a red sea spread over the prairie. At five thousand feet, houses, barns, churches, trucks, cars, naval rescue craft, soldiers and sailors, were little toys scattered around a giant brown mud puddle. I had previously thought of floods as thundering and dramatic but this was more like the water rising slowly and inexorably up in your bathtub and overflowing your house with no way to drain it.

On "Black Friday," May 5, the Red River silently destroyed dikes and invaded thousands of homes, including my own. There was a plan to evacuate all of the city should the river rise much more, but fortunately on May 25, with almost a quarter of the city under five feet of water, the muddy flood began to recede. Meantime, 100,000 people had fled and the flood had damaged 10,500 Winnipeg homes. A generation later the mighty flood barrier was erected.

During my year and a half in the West I learned about the other half of my "unknown country." It was a time when Alberta's Leduc oil field was attracting American investment and stimulating the modernization of the prairies. I rode steam harvesters as big as dinosaurs in northern Saskatchewan, attended Ukrainian weddings, and spent a mountain-walking weekend at Banff Springs Hotel amid peaks that deserve that abused word "awesome." On a CPR train travelling through the buttes, bluffs, sandstone outcrops and lunar rock formations called hoodoos in the Alberta badlands, I also saw the last of the Old West. In a scene from a Frederic Remington painting, an Indian in feathered head dress, mounted on a pony with his family around him, was silhouetted in the setting sun on a little hill, watching the train pass by. What a different place Canada was in those days.

That autumn of 1950 I received the letter from London I had long been hoping for. If I were prepared to pay my own way to get there, I could have a job with the European Division of United Press, based in London. After nearly six years of covering Canadian news, Margaret and I took the train to Quebec City and embarked on a ship for England.

7

WARM BEER, COLD COMFORT

London in December 1950 was bleak, cold, shabby and hungry. "You'd think we'd lost the bloody war," a taxi driver complained. Sugar, butter, meat and clothing were rationed. The people who'd danced in the streets on VE-Day were nostalgic for the comradeship and adrenalin of the Blitz although it had killed 30,000 Londoners.

If Britain's Age of Austerity was pure misery for the British, it was pure adventure for us fresh from the bland abundance of post-war Canada. Romantic fog and poverty were the stuff of Sherlock Holmes, David Copperfield and George Orwell's "gloomy Sundays, smoky towns, and red pillar-boxes." Margaret and I disembarked from the *Franconia* into cold, smoky Liverpool, which was like a black and white movie set, and boarded the little toy train with its grubby compartments and no interior access to a toilet. Schoolboys came aboard in short pants, knee socks and chilblains. There were few cars on the roads. The fishmongers, chemists, tobacconists, green grocers and ominous-sounding "family butchers" with whole carcasses on steel hooks had changed little since Queen Victoria's death. That evening at the Trocadero restaurant "in the heart of the Empire" we dined off turnip soup, beefless Beef Wellington, bread pudding and watery ale. Raised on cosy English lore and the BBC Empire service, we were happy just to be in Piccadilly Circus.

On Monday we searched for an apartment in the city where Nazi bombers had destroyed more property than the Great Fire of 1666. Streets which had been crowded since the reign of Henry VIII were covered in rubble and the weeds called London Pride. Few homes had been built for six years but on elegant Regent's Park Crescent

Margaret found a three-room furnished flat that had suffered bomb damage which made the floors squeak. It seemed cheap at £10 a week until someone told us that the average English wage was £150 a year and first division football players made £12 a week. There was no central heating and at four o'clock on Christmas Eve we ran out of shillings for the metered gas fire and the explosive geyser which heated our water.

Christmas morning was damp and cold with frost underfoot in the silent, empty streets. Restaurants were closed but not the pubs with their ornamental mirrors, cast-iron fireplaces and dark wood-work, where beer was warm and Scotch whisky cheap. Just before closing time on Christmas Eve we bought bottles of whiskey at the off-licence bar, having failed to purchase proper Christmas presents because the shops had closed early. Out on the street our friend Mike, who had tucked a bottle under his right arm, raised his hand to hail a taxi and the bottle splintered on the pavement. It was that sort of Christmas.

January produced an influenza epidemic, power failures and a powdering of snow. The city smelled of coal fires and soot. We queued for horse meat, whale meat and strange tinned South African fish called *snoek*. We rode the red double-deck buses and the dirty Underground, whose rumbling tunnels had been communal bed-rooms filled with fearful humanity during the worst air raids.

There were few taken-for-granted North American amenities: no supermarkets, tea bags, sliced bread, frozen food, washing machines or microwaves. As a result of what would now be regarded as dep-rivations, the British were actually healthier than before the war, the government having had the sense to ensure proper nutrition for all; moreover, the new National Health Service owned the hospi-tals, employed 90 per cent of the doctors and provided free medical and dental care. Londoners were more civil to each other than they are now and there was more offering of seats on buses and trains.

With the British Broadcasting Corporation acting as the arbiter of conduct, Victorian taboos forbade raunchy references over the air to honeymoons, prostitution, lavatories, male effeminacy, chambermaids, commercial travellers, underwear, fig leaves and rabbits. Which is not to imply that the land of Chaucer and Shakespeare had lost all sense of bawdy humour or had discarded amiable rural signposts like North Piddle (Worcestershire), Titty Ho (Northamptonshire), Pratts Bottom (Kent) or Butthole Road (Yorkshire).

Pubs usually had sufficient best bitter to drown the taste of ersatz hamburgers made from oatmeal and potatoes, or meatless Scotch eggs, which were hard-boiled, coated in breadcrumbs and deep-fried. Five shillings bought a meal of soup, bubble-and-squeak, rock cod and chips or whale steaks and jam roly-poly. Music halls and Christmas pantomimes – *Babes in the Wood, Mother Goose* and *Aladdin* – were sold out, as were dog races and football matches. We saw T. S. Eliot's *The Cocktail Party* and Christopher Fry's *The Lady's Not for Burning* and some of England's best-ever movies: *Brief Encounter, Kind Hearts and Coronets, The Third Man, Odd Man Out, Great Expectations, Hamlet*.

Our United Press offices were in the *News of the World* building on Bouverie Street, between the Thames Embankment and Fleet Street, where Tudor facades clashed with the modern grey austerity of the *Daily Telegraph* and the art deco black glass of Beaverbrook's *Daily Express*. British newspapers had retained the practice of filling their front pages with advertisements and burying the news inside as they had for generations. "Here rumours and gossip from all the world come pouring in," wrote a 19th-century historian, "and from this echoing hall are reverberated back in strangely modified form." It seemed nothing much had changed. It was pleasant to imagine the local pubs had known Shakespeare, Pepys and Dr. Johnson.

Before newspapers moved east into dockland, "the Street" smelled of ink, warm newsprint and motor exhaust and was so crowded at night I preferred going to work at dawn when the sounds and smells were the seagulls from the river and Cockney cleaning ladies in head scarves rattling buckets of soapsuds and puffing Woodbines. At 6 a.m it was still barely possible to imagine Wordworth's "visionary scene – a length of street / Laid open in its morning quietness."

My first news story broke as I was starting a dawn shift on Christmas Day and Scotland Yard announced the theft of the irreplaceable Stone of Scone from Westminster Abbey. The Yard provided few details: the stone weighed 300 pounds, measured 16 by 10 inches, had been used in British coronations for centuries, and the police were watching roads leading north because Scots nationalists were the likely suspects. Government offices being closed for the holidays, I had only our inadequate reference library to help me tease out details; the missing relic was a quasi-religious artifact of rough sandstone that had been used for the coronation of Scottish kings long before it was captured from the Abbey of Scone near Perth by Edward I of England and carried off to London in 1296, where, embedded under the throne like a chamber pot, it had served at English coronations ever since. It was months before we learned that the culprits were four Glasgow students who had hidden it in rocky terrain, where it looked like the other rocks, before lugging it off to Scotland in somebody's car. After it turned up on the altar of Scotland's abandoned Arbroath Abbey in April it was returned to Westminster to play a part in the coronation of Queen Elizabeth II. The students were arrested but never charged.

In a news agency – UP, AP, Reuters or France Presse – with thousands of clients around the world the work meant not only chasing headlines but being ready to cover any subject under the sun at any time whether politics, the arts, crime, commerce, fashion, sports or human oddities. Perhaps because I was Canadian I was assigned an international ski jumping meet on the green slopes of London's Hampstead Heath. It rained, but snow trucked in from the Welsh

Dubbed the "Street of Adventure" by journalist Sir Phillip Gibbs and the "Street of Shame" for its tabloids, Fleet Street was a centre of publishing for five centuries until newspapers were dispersed to other locations in the 1970s and '80s.

mountains to cover the wooden piste lasted long enough for the Norwegians to win and our clients in Oslo to be pleased.

Springtime in England being so rarely what poets imagine, April was cold and rainy but the skeletal forest of cranes on the south bank of the Thames promised a brighter future as the Festival of Britain took shape. For the opening of the 1951 Festival on May 3 two thousand fires were lit around the country and a forty-one-gun salute was fired from the Tower of London. After a service attended by Queen Elizabeth and Princesses Elizabeth and Margaret, the ailing King

George stood before a flag-waving crowd at the steps of St. Paul's Cathedral and declared the festival open.

The long-awaited showcase of Britain's arts, sciences and technology suddenly redeemed the chill, wet days with a burst of colour and design. According to my rain-stained, dog-eared notes of half a century ago, the Festival was built on twenty-seven acres of bomb site. Winston Churchill, ousted from office by the Labour Party, was at the opening, damp and grumpy, and telling people the festival was socialist propaganda. When his Conservatives regained power later that year all the buildings except the Royal Festival Hall were torn down. As with any box of delights, the excitement lay in the packaging. After twelve years of war and austerity, ration books, powdered eggs and "going without," people began to smile. Among 15,000 exhibits the ones I liked best were the futuristic Dome of Discovery with its 300-foot sculpted needle of steel and aluminum, and The Lion and the Unicorn pavilion, a whimsical celebration of Englishness, featuring Punch and Alice in Wonderland and the White Knight.

Postwar London had been grey, broken and dirty with no money for paint and repairs but here was this stylish, colourful showplace with always something new. Not far away Battersea Park, transformed into the Festival Gardens with elevated tree walks, fountains and a grotto, entranced a nation starved of fun. There was open-air dancing and when it rained people brought umbrellas and danced the Hokey Cokey in their raincoats. Rationing was relaxed and people ate roast beef again and Neapolitan wafer ice-creams with wedges of strawberry, vanilla and chocolate.

Margaret and I were at the Festival one afternoon when a distinguished-looking man in typical dark suit, derby and carrying a rolled umbrella spoke to us. Expecting London gentlemen to be constitutionally aloof, we were surprised by his friendliness until we discovered he was a Scot, an army major in mufti who had served in Ottawa and recognized our accents. When I mentioned we were going to the Edinburgh Festival, he suggested we travel on to the Highlands and make use of his ancestral home, where there was a housekeeper, although he could not be there himself. We accepted with pleasure.

One morning in August we boarded the black and red Flying Scotsman at King's Cross and seven hours later steamed into Waverley Station in time to climb the steep road to Edinburgh Castle to the Military Tattoo with its massed pipe bands. Following the advice of Robert Louis Stevenson, we found that the best views, stretching from Leith to Arthur's Seat and Salisbury Crags, were seen from Calton Hill, at the east of Princes Street. In one of the most beautiful cities of the world we ate haggis, explored the Royal Mile, and attended concerts and Ewan MacColl's anti-war *Uranium 235* at the Edinburgh Festival.

We rode a clattery pre-war bus up the coast to Inverness and on to our new friend's house, Kilvannie in the Great Glen. Mrs. Mackenzie, the motherly housekeeper, delighted to meet Scots Canadians, suggested we visit Boleskine House, once home of the recently dead Aleister Crowley, author and Satanist. Such was Crowley's reputation as the Great Beast of the Book of Revelations that tradesmen still treated his house like Dracula's Castle and refused to deliver. Finding little to scare us at Boleskine House, however, we spent most of the day searching for the Loch Ness monster, reputedly seen by another couple named MacKay, owners of nearby Drumnadrochit Hotel. According to the *Inverness Courier* they had been travelling the southeast shore of the loch in 1933 when they saw "an enormous animal rolling and plunging" in the water. There had been so many alleged sightings since then that Nessie competes for crypto-zoology popularity with the Abominable Snowman and Bigfoot. Loch Ness is a freshwater lake about 750 feet deep, twenty-four miles long and between a mile and a mile and a half wide, and at dusk as we were biking back to eat Mrs. Mackenzie's dinner we saw, or thought we saw, an undulating shape far out in the water. We returned in the morning and watched well into the evening but saw nothing of interest. I have recently read that sonar gear has detected "animate targets" twenty feet long in the lower depths. The myth refuses to die.

Back in London we spent happy weekends exploring Thames estuary towns and the fens and marshes of East Anglia. When the Festival of Britain closed its doors in September a choir of school children sang "Together we'll build tomorrow today." The British had seen a world brighter, better designed, less regimented but the Labour government that had brought them this holiday from drabness lost the election. Prime Minister Clement Atlee, a decent, unimposing man, had fought poverty, disease and ignorance through social and economic reforms, nationalizing railroads, public utilities, heavy industry and the Bank of England. His government had created the welfare state, free health care, unemployment and retirement benefits and free education. But young Margaret Roberts, the grocer's daughter soon to be Margaret Thatcher, was not alone in complaining it was "pernicious" and destructive of British character. The changes had been too radical and the task of government fell to the Conservatives, led once more by Winston Churchill.

During the five-week election campaign I took the train one evening to Churchill's constituency in Woodford, Essex, on the northern fringe of London. Churchill's wife, Clementine, had tried to dissuade him from running, the Labour party had called him a war-monger, and at the age of seventy-six he was stooped and showing his years, but he promised the small room full of supporters to lead "a strong and free Britain."

"There lies before us now a difficult time, a hard time," he said. "I do not doubt we shall come through because we shall use not only our party forces but a growing sense of the need to put Britain back in her place – a need which burns in the hearts of men far beyond these shores." Voted into office in October 1951 on a platform of lower taxes and denationalization, "Good old Winnie" was challenged by rising prices, unemployment, inadequate housing and the onset of the Cold War.

Meantime, the conditions producing London's notorious yellow smog since the 17th century – fog mixed with smoke, soot and sulphur trapped by temperature inversion – seemed less romantic to us than when we had arrived. In December a killer smog, invading theatres, cinemas and restaurants, stung our eyes and noses and turned people across the room into ghosts.

A week before Christmas I was fighting a cold, anticipating flu and putting on my coat to go home one dim afternoon when the European editor asked if I'd like to manage the bureau in Lisbon. The manager for thirty years, a Portuguese, had apparently left under a cloud, no one seemed to have any details, and the urgency was due to the fact that an important NATO conference was soon to be held there. If I accepted I would depart within a week, which meant that Margaret would follow after disposing of our rented flat.

Portugal not being the tourist destination it is now, we knew little about the country except that it enjoyed a mild seaside climate, was ruled by a dictator and possessed colonies in Africa and Asia. Someone who had been there on holiday said it was known for "three F's – football, Fado and Fatima." But with smog obscuring our windows we had visions of sunny days, beaches and Goethe's southern haven "where lemon trees blossom, golden oranges glow and a gentle breeze from blue skies drifts."

I bought a Portuguese-English dictionary and acquired a visa, which I noticed bore the stamp of the political police, the PIDE *(Policia International e Defesa de Estado)*. I had no idea that in the next few years I would be reporting on the demise of the world's oldest empire.

8

WHERE THE BLUE BEGINS

Somewhere over southern France our Portuguese DC-3 flew out of the dark rain clouds into an afternoon of ethereal southern blue. The new Heathrow terminal had been grey and cold, the Pyrenees capped with snow, but Spain on this last day of 1951 was a warm-tan carpet of silent plains and honey-hued towns, the green hills of Portugal a sunnier Wales. Since I was used only to trains and ships – and distances measured in days rather than hours – the afternoon was an unaccustomed leap from English winter into a virtual spring.

The Portuguese capital in the pale gold afternoon looked clean and whole on its seven hills, a Ruritanian rarity compared with battered London. Yellow and brown trams rolled down the edges of wide boulevards past statues of 16th-century explorers and stolid, five-storey buildings painted powder blue, ochre, dove grey or pale green. Gaily coloured washing flapped from balconies in the Atlantic breeze and a rooster crowed in a courtyard. On mosaic sidewalks of polished black and white small stones were cafés thronged with men.

The Aviz Hotel, a creamy stucco mansion with black trim, was a former royal palace converted by the Rugeroni family from Gibraltar into a twenty-room bijou with three servants for every guest and a garden where there were peacocks and, yes, "lemon trees blossomed and golden oranges glowed." I describe it here in some detail because it no longer exists in that form, but in its time the Aviz was arguably the best small hotel in the world. The fanciful elevator which took us to the second floor was fashioned from an 18th-century royal coach, with pink plush seats, windows with gold-fringed velvet curtains and a gilt door. During World War II the Aviz was frequented by German and English spies but the best suite was occupied then as now by Calouste Gulbenkian, an Anglo-Armenian philanthropist who fled Paris to escape the Nazis after making his fortune in 5 per cent commissions in Middle East oil.

While I was checking in, Mr. Five Percent himself walked through the lobby, short-legged, bald, bushy-browed, followed by secretary, valet and chauffeur, a rooster followed by chicks. Unexpectedly, my boss, A.L. Bradford, also appeared, having flown in from his base in Paris, not something normally done when a junior staffer was starting an assignment. I was curious as to what he had in mind. That evening I met Bradford and his wife, an elegant Montenegrin princess, in the Aviz restaurant, where Gulbenkian was eating his frugal supper on a little dais in the corner, presumably so he could command a view of the whole room. We, however, celebrated New Year's Eve with an expense account dinner of stuffed crab, roast partridge, asparagus, tree-fresh oranges and pineapples, vintage wine and cognac. I noticed that while United Press reporters were forever being warned to stint, salesmen like Bradford spent lavishly on entertainment.

A.L Bradford, United Press vice-president for Europe, the Middle East and Africa, was a tall, white-haired patrician Virginian known for both charm and a bullying temper. I was here, he told me, because the press credentials of my predecessor, Adolfo Viera DaRosa, had been abruptly revoked on orders from Prime Minister António de Oliveira Salazar. History was repeating itself, for the same thing had happened to DaRosa's predecessor in the 1920s. I wondered if it would one day happen to me. This being a dictatorship, Bradford feared United Press itself would be banned from the country, if not forever at least for the duration of the seminal conference of the North Atlantic Treaty Organisation (NATO) to be held in Lisbon (or *Lish-boa* as we learned to call it). Bradford had a second agenda, which was only later revealed. Portugal being virtually the only country in western Europe where UP had failed to sell its world news service, he had arranged a meeting with Premier Salazar to lobby for government support in introducing our service to the Portuguese media. He had done something similar in Franco Spain, selling the service to the government-controlled EFE agency, which put United Press in the position of depending on income from a government which censored newspapers and radio stations and banned labour unions.

Bradford and his wife had retired for the night and I was with a friend in the Aviz bar when a bellboy handed me an envelope bearing the stamp of the Secretariado da Informação, the ministry of propaganda. I spoke no Portuguese, had no idea where our two local employees might be on New Year's Eve, or even where they lived, so was at a loss until my friend, who happened to be a Reuters Madrid correspondent visiting Lisbon on holiday, came to my rescue and translated the communiqué, which announced an abortive coup against the Salazar government. Without his help I would have been ignominiously scooped on my first night in town while my boss, who wished to impress the Portuguese with UP's competence, slumbered peacefully upstairs.

On New Year's Day the Bradfords took me sight-seeing in their chauffeured hired car, a mild, sunny afternoon spent at Gothic palaces, baroque churches with painted ceilings, medieval castles, the pale pink Queluz Palace, a miniature Versailles, the fantasy spires of Pena Palace in Sintra, and the Estoril Riviera, home to exiled kings and queens of half a dozen countries.

After Bradford left for Paris next day I booked into a much more modest hotel and walked down palm-lined Avenida da Liberdade, past the gardens and open-air cafés and many shoe-shine boys, to the Secretariado da Informação in the pink stucco Palácio Foz on

Graced by trees, gardens and open-air cafés, the heart of Lisbon was Avenida da Liberdade, Praça dos Restauradores and the Rossio, the latter thick with people, confectioners, shoeshine boys, newspaper and tobacco kiosks.

Praça dos Restauradores. A plump, avuncular former ship's physician, a bachelor and bon vivant unaccountably in charge of foreign press relations, smoked cigarettes in a long amber holder and issued press credentials and worldly advice.

Our office was in the Baixa, or lower town, where medieval streets were named for their businesses, rua do Ouro (Gold) and rua da Prata (Silver). On the second floor of an old building, our UP office contained two worn desks, two telephones, a rusty electric heater to ward off morning chill and two middle-aged *journalistas* who physically, though not otherwise, resembled Stan Laurel and Oliver Hardy. Senhor José was stout, well-meaning and spoke, but could not write, understandable English. Senhor António was a small, lean *"alfacinha,"* or "little lettuce eater," as Lisbon people were called, who professed to know no English at all and from his secretive manner might have been a spy for the ubiquitous PIDE police though

I eventually learned to trust him. There was a raggedy office boy whose packed lunches perfumed the office with stale fish in rancid olive oil. The staff were understandably anxious about their new boss and their future; as a twenty-six-year-old foreigner who didn't speak their language, I didn't blame them. In a country where age took weighty precedence over callow youth, it took time and effort to win their confidence.

My predecessor, DaRosa, had been UP's second Lisbon manager, hired in the 1920s after a man named Eugene Pilgrim had suffered imprisonment followed by expulsion for reporting the views of banned left-wing parties. In a hotly competitive business that valued innovative ways of speeding the news, DaRosa was known for having begun his tenure with a journalistic coup which involved the un-authorized purchase of half a dozen shotguns to, of all things, report on some aviators who were vying to be the first to fly the South Atlantic. A Swiss pilot bound for South America had suddenly decided to take off one Sunday morning from a remote pasture. The nearest telephone being miles away in the village of Villa Franca, DaRosa supplied five farmers with shotguns and stationed them on hills at suitable intervals between plane and village. When he saw the plane take off, he fired his shotgun and the sound was relayed across the hills, shot after shot, to the village, where an assistant was waiting to phone New York UP, beating the Associated Press and Reuters.

Margaret arrived and we began setting up housekeeping, as we had previously done in Halifax, Montreal, Winnipeg and London. We rented a large flat on the top floor of a five-storey, mustard-coloured 19th-century building with wrought-iron balconies over-looking the harbour, where tan-sailed boats brought rural produce down the Tagus. Our little street, reached by the free-standing Santa Justa elevator, which resembled the Eiffel Tower, contained a cosy little bar run by an elderly White Russian called Fred who played his guitar and sang sad Slavic songs. There was no central heating in our flat so we spent many hours that winter at Fred's or down the street at the Pastelaria-Padaria São Roque, a café-bakery where we ate coconut-topped *pão de deus* – the bread of god.

While studying our language books Margaret and I thrust our legs beneath the satin skirts of a circular table which hid a brazier, which was how Portuguese had coped with winter for centuries, though ours was heated by electricity rather than charcoal. When our first daughter was born in 1954 during the only Lisbon snowstorm in memory, our housekeeper, a motherly white-haired former ship's stewardess named Olympia,

The neo-Gothic Elevador de Santa Justa, 140 feet high, designed at the end of the 19th century by a protégé of Gustave Eiffel, contained two large elevators which connected the Baixa or the lower town with Bairro Alto, where we lived.

suggested we name her Branca da Neve – Snow White. We named her Marina. Our younger daughter, Karen, was born in 1956 in more salubrious weather.

With Olympia's help we learned the medieval economics of the small, dark shops of baker, butcher and gull-voiced *varinhas* or fishwives with naked feet and flat baskets of silver *sardinhas* on their heads. A city of the sea, Lisbon was famous for fish restaurants whose menus ascended from a tasty cod dish, *brandade de bacalhau,* through superb sole to gourmet dressed crab. Anything involving local labour – domestic service, custom-made suit, wine, a fish, a loaf of bread – was cheap. Anything imported – ketchup, corn flakes, aspirin, Kleenex – was an expensive luxury. Having been bypassed by the Industrial Revolution, the country depended mostly on grapes, grain, cork, fish, almonds and olives We joined the expatriate community of British, American, French with whom we drank, played tennis, swam, sailed and attended bull fights in which matadors refrained from killing the bull. This for me was a symbolic difference between Spain and Portugal, also reflected in music. Spain had its wild, harsh flamenco, Portugal the soft, forlorn fado of nostalgic, yearning and untranslatable *"saudades"* as rendered by Amalia Rodrigues, a beautiful woman born in poverty in the shadowy narrow streets of Alfama below the battlements of Castelo de San Jorge.

Although some consider the Portuguese language difficult, we found it easier than, say, French though I wished I had learned more Latin in school, Portuguese being a stepchild of the Latin spoken during the Roman Iberian occupation. Our chief difficulty was pronunciation of the accented nasal "ão" dipthong which creates an almost inaudible "n" sound whereby São (as in São Paulo) sounds more like *sow-n* rather than *say-o*. Another challenge was the Portuguese "s", which sounds like a leaky tire. We became used to flowery speech wherein shopkeepers and waiters addressed us as *Vossa Excelência* and anyone with some education as *Senhor Doutor* or *Senhor Engenheiro*. Pale, scholarly, bespectacled Senhor Trindade came twice a week to teach grammar. As for the rest, such as the difference between appearance and reality in Salazar's Portugal, we had to learn by ourselves.

Portugal was my first live-in encounter with an entirely new culture, my first attempt to report the news from a police state, a country where there was hardly any middle class and the repressed population eked out a meagre living as tenant farmers and labourers in a world of inadequate housing, poor health care and illiteracy.

Half the towns lacked electricity and running water. Per capita income was half that of Spain and Portuguese were emigrating in large numbers to France, Britain, America and Canada.

Since the 1920s Salazar had been running a one-party state supported by an oligarchy of the military and rich families, sanctified by the Catholic Church. Much of rural Portugal consisted of estates controlled by a tiny upper class that had claimed them during the reconquest of the peninsula from the Moors. A professor of economics at Coimbra University, Salazar had been recruited by the army to save Portugal from bankruptcy after sixteen years of revolutions and short-lived governments. He had promised peace and a balanced budget but in delivering the latter at the expense of the former had been the target of two failed assassinations and six unsuccessful coups. As the Spanish philosopher Miguel Unamuno wrote, Portugal was "outwardly gentle and smiling but tormented and tragic within."

Salazar's Union National Party was modelled on Mussolini's Fascist Corporate State, its corporations and syndicates run by an Old Boy network of supporters. Unlike Mussolini, Salazar avoided overt bullyboy tactics although his Gestapo-trained PIDE made arrests without warrants and held prisoners without charge. Not that Salazar looked like a dictator. He was soft-spoken, devout, his face priest-

like and care-worn. He had trained for the priesthood, wore dark suits and elastic-sided boots and lived a quiet, abstemious life attended by an adoring housekeeper. Despite his disdain for

Antonio de Oliveira Salazar, economist and university professor, ruled with modest despotism and, somewhat like the Wonderful Wizard of Oz, fostered the illusion he was the only person in the world able to solve the country's problems.

democracy, his regime was widely regarded abroad as benign. The Americans were content to have an avid anti-communist ally in the Cold War and a British diplomat observed that "if Salazar ruled his fellow-countrymen severely he did on the whole rule them well." Many Portuguese would have disagreed had they dared. Their pent-up frustrations were to surface in the surprisingly peaceful revolution of 1974.

My immediate reason for being in Lisbon in the winter of 1952 was a five-day NATO conference chaired by Canada's foreign affairs minister, Lester B. Pearson. The travelling circus called the international press corps was there, roustabouts from the wire services and the high-wire performers from the *New York Times, Le Monde* and *The Times* of London. Randolph Churchill, on assignment for the *Daily Telegraph*, spent a lot of time in the bar, where he was overheard to say his famous father, then seventy-eight, was having severe memory problems. The American-led North Atlantic Treaty Organization was then in its formative stage, fourteen countries brought together by fear of a Soviet push into western Europe and the almost constant danger of nuclear war. "An armed attack against one shall be considered an attack against all," NATO declared, and the Lisbon meeting provided twenty-five battle-ready divisions with another twenty in reserve.

That spring I also covered the annual international pilgrimage to the Shrine of Fatima, where three shepherd children claimed in 1917 to have seen a ghostly woman who advised them to pray for the salvation of Communist Russia, a country they had never heard of. That Fatima was a fairy tale promoted by the Vatican seemed irrelevant when I saw crowds of poor, afflicted, hopeful women literally crawling on their knees toward the statue of Our Lady of Fatima.

In those days, before the Portuguese empire imploded, Lisbon was not a major news centre, but since I was the only person in the bureau who could write English I had to be ready at all hours when news did break – a failed coup, the unexpected death of a royal exile, a bloody riot in the colonies, a plane hijacking, the six jet fighter planes which unaccountably came crashing down, one after the other, into the Estrella Mountains one morning as I was about to leave the office for lunch.

With five thousand clients around the world, we often received special requests, as when the always-debonair Anthony Eden, Britain's fifty-five-year-old foreign secretary and soon-to-be prime minister, married Winston Churchill's thirty-two-year-old niece, Clarissa Spencer-Churchill, and the *Daily Express* in London demanded I provide "blanket coverage" of their honeymoon at a small rural hotel. It wanted gossip, but the best I could manage was the pedestrian news that the bride had left her cosmetic case in London and it had to be flown out to her, or the less-than-earthshaking fact that post-war currency restrictions had allowed them only £25 each, so they spent the last weekend of their honeymoon as penniless guests in the British embassy.

I was occasionally called on to work in Spain and in May 1954 covered the visit of Queen Elizabeth and Prince Philip to Gibraltar to commemorate the 250th anniversary of the British occupation of that disputed Pillar of Hercules. When the visit was announced, Spain had objected so vehemently there were fears it would become the occasion for terrorism. One British newspaper reported the 27,000 residents and servicemen on "the Rock" were so fanatically loyal they would "tear to pieces" anyone with evil designs. That, apparently, was enough of a guarantee of Her Majesty's safety for the visit to go ahead. During walkabouts by the Queen, Prince Philip and small Prince Charles and Princess Anne, the locals were tremendously welcoming, as were the 230 Barbary macaques, or apes, which the royal party visited in the lofty nature reserve. There was a legend that if the apes should leave, Britain would have to leave too, so everyone, including Prince Philip, was nice to them. Philip was not so nice when a press photographer trying for a fancy shot of the royal family fell off a telephone pole, for I heard him utter something rude and uncomplimentary about the photographer's neck in his bluff Royal Naval way. Thankfully for all of us the young Queen's visit passed without incident but it was the cause of Franco's renewed efforts to reclaim Gibraltar for Spain.

*   *   *

In the 1950s Salazar began showing a somewhat more progressive face, which is to say he encouraged foreign investment and industrial development and the building of power dams, roads and airports. Reluctantly promoting the mass tourism that was to change the feudal countryside, he converted impoverished Algarve into a major tourist attraction with travel posters which declared "Portugal is Europe's best kept secret – quaint, unspoiled and cheap."

When Margaret and I first visited the Algarve in 1952 to see the February almond blossoms, our accommodation was the little Pensão Solar Penguin which stood above the golden beach of Praia da Rocha, a B&B run eccentrically by two retired Scots bankers named Stewart and James, where we vacationed for five dollars a day including meals with wine and cheap gin in gallon containers. Within a few years the government converted the empty beaches of the Algarve into the overcrowded international playground it is today.

To report on touristic developments on the subtropical island of Madeira, Margaret and I made a four-day trip with two young Canadians from Vancouver who were sailing from England to South America in a miniature version of a 25-ton Brixton trawler. She had an auxiliary motor for getting in and out of harbour, but her sails, spars and everything else were 19th century, heavy and awkward. Sailing "wing and wing" – sails spread on both sides – with the wind behind us we logged 120 miles a day but since we were navigating by dead reckoning, on the fourth day we almost missed Madeira

Old and awkward, a retired fishing boat from Brixton, Devon, while no luxury yacht, carried us under sail in a steady east-west wind from this mooring in Lisbon to the semi-tropical mid-Atlantic island of Madeira.

and were on our way to South America when we noticed a small cloud behind us which could only signify land. We had to tack upwind for some considerable time to get into Funchal harbour. After exploring the white town up the steep slope from the harbour and discovering the uniquely high-temperature process by which dark, sweet fortified Madeira wine is made, Margaret and I returned to Lisbon on the Royal Mail liner *Alcantara,* which plied between South America and the UK. While sailing to Madeira on our little trawler I'd had to crawl into the toilet in the cramped bow on hands and knees, often half asleep in the middle of the night. Which explains why Margaret found me at 1 a.m. on the *Alcantara* crawling along a red-carpeted corridor in my sleep, fortunately before anyone else encountered me.

Portugal's original tourist attraction had been Estoril's casino, hotels, beaches and race track, where exiled kings and queens maintained miniature courts as if they were real rulers. At the weekly round of embassy cocktail parties they were not unlike the rest of us, nibbling party food and drinking wine or whisky. The richest, I suppose, was King Carol of Rumania, a playboy who married his voluptuous red-haired mistress Magda Lupescu, the Catholic daughter of a Jewish chemist. While looking forward to interviewing King Carol I was awakened by a phone call from New York around 3 a.m. on an Easter Saturday to learn something a wire-service reporter never wants to hear. The *New York Times* had a front-page story from the opposition – Reuters in this case – reporting the king's death. Carol had died the previous night of a heart attack at the age of sixty-one after a game of tennis, and my paid contact in the royal household had failed us; since there was only one phone line into the royal home and it remained busy, it was impossible to confirm the report until we got our own staffer to the house half an hour away in the middle of the night. It was no comfort that AP and Agence France Presse had also missed the story or that the Reuters correspondent, a medical doctor as well as a journalist, had been lucky. A bachelor who suffered from insomnia, he was in a bar at midnight when the king's doctor happened by for a nightcap and told him Carol had just died.

When Frank Bartholomew, president of United Press, arrived on a tour of inspection from New York, because he owned a vineyard in California I took him to a winery. A guide with a flashlight was showing Frank, the new European vice-president Tom Curran, and me around a vast dark cellar where white wine was fermented in tanks set into the floor when his light winked out. In the dark I stepped into an open manhole. The fermenting wine stank but the tank was so shallow I was able to scramble out. My new summer suit was ruined and sticky and, driving back to Lisbon with them on that hot August afternoon, I smelled of advanced fermentation, a rank cabbage smell reminiscent of an oil refinery. It would have been safer to have taken them to Estoril.

Estoril was the place where Salazar relaxed in a former seaside fort decorated with images of the 16th-century adventurers who had founded a global empire twenty times bigger than metropolitan Portugal that stretched halfway around the world from east Timor and Macao to the Azores and Madeira and included Goa and the nation-sized colonies of Angola and Mozambique.

Obsessed with the belief that Portugal's future lay in Angola with its diamond mines and oil, Salazar dreamed of recreating a "new Brazil" to replace the colony that had broken away in 1810. Though by the 1950s the British, French and Belgians already were abandoning their colonies, Salazar was determined to stay – the last of the old empires – with the help of the United States and South Africa. He nationalized the colonial railways and ports and subsidized the white planters of coffee, sugar, tea and cocoa. In a transparent bid for international goodwill he changed the names associated with white domination. Colonies became "overseas provinces," the ministry of colonies became the "overseas ministry," colonial governors became provincial governors general. At the same time, the government began cracking down on any hint of African separatism. In Lisbon, African students who so much as formed a cultural society were accused of anti-colonialism. The Angolan poet and medical student Agostinho Neto, son of a black Methodist minister, was imprisoned and accused of communism.

That Salazar's opponents were not all "communists and anarchists" Margaret and I discovered when we made friends with a red-haired neighbour in our apartment building. She was the mistress of Captain Henrique Galvão, who had been jailed when his clandestine Organização Civica Nacional was infiltrated by the secret police. Galvão was later to escape and make world headlines in 1961 by kidnapping the Portuguese cruise liner *Santa Maria* in an effort to publicize the evils of forced labour in Portugal's African colonies. Once a trusted Salazar supporter, Galvão had been Inspector General of Colonial Administration when he fell afoul of his patron by calling the government's African forced labour policy what it was – slavery. Although Galvão ended his days in exile in Brazil, having failed to sail the *Santa Maria* to Luanda to establish an alternative government, his quixotic deeds did a lot to spark the revolt that set off Angola's long war of liberation.

Although I had been responsible for coverage of the Portuguese African and Asian colonies, I'd not been able to travel there, but in 1954 I got my chance. Bradford had succeeded in his three-year campaign to sell the UP service to the government-controlled Portuguese news agency ANI. Now having some bureau income with which to pay for such journeys, I was also able to hire an assistant who could write English, namely John Marks, an author and former Madrid correspondent for *The Times* of London who had recently moved to Portugal.

Despite the virtually impenetrable censorship of news of Portuguese Africa, we had been hearing rumours from the little colony of São Tomé on the Gulf of Guinea about a massacre of rebellious black indentured labourers sent from Angola to work in the cocoa fields. Now having someone to run the bureau in my absence, I applied for a visa and in April 1954 I got a yellow fever shot.

9

THE LOST EMPIRE

Far below in vast African darkness tiny bush fires flickered like fireflies. Shortly before dawn our Pan American Constellation, en route from Lisbon to Johannesburg, made the first of two scheduled landings in West Africa.

I wrote in my travel diary: "April 3, 1954, Roberts Field, Liberia: 4 a.m. Sticky heat, smoky African smells of herbs and damp earth. A dimly lit terminal shed, shadows, shiny black faces. An American from the Firestone rubber plantation told me the descendants of the freed American slaves who founded the Liberian republic in the 19th century continue to impose slavery on bush tribes. While we were taking off at dawn a tall half-naked man with a tribal head dress arose out of the elephant grass beside the runway like the ghost of an older Africa.

"April 4, 1954 Leopoldville: 90 humid degrees (F) at 9 a.m. A bustling divided city with modern office blocks and pale Belgians in dark business suits or flowered European dresses who live in ranch-style homes on palm-lined boulevards in the neighbourhood called Kinshasa. Blacks are segregated in a township beyond the park and golf course where they remain at night under eight-hour curfew. The Belgians insist Congo independence is decades away, but the Canadian Trade Commissioner told me independence is coming sooner and won't be pretty."

A small Portuguese plane took me southwest across equatorial jungle, thinly wooded highlands, broken hills, scattered coffee plantations and down a coastal plain with long vistas of empty Atlantic beaches.

"April 7 Luanda: This handsome old capital seems almost European. The 55,000 white people within the city out-number blacks who live in surrounding shantytowns. All work of consequence is done by whites. Even hotel waiters are white, unusual in colonial Africa. A keen young government official has come to the hotel (to keep an eye on me?) with a list of places and people."

My bureaucratic visitor gave me literature describing how the Bantu kingdom of King Ngola was settled by Portuguese in 1575 when a hundred families from Lisbon arrived with a detachment of soldiers. "There's no colour bar," he earnestly assured me. "No one has better relations with natives than us Portuguese and the natives are grateful." When blacks became educated and "assimilated" they could own property, he said, but he conceded that the relatively few *"assimilados"* were in effect second-class citizens who must carry

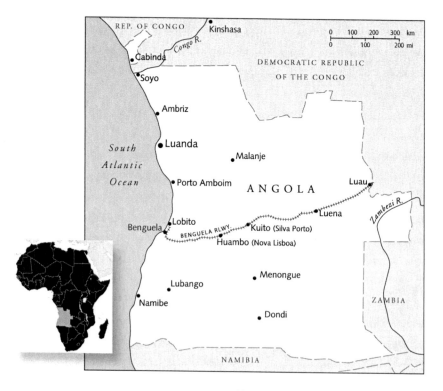

identity cards and were paid less than whites or mulattos. While he insisted the Portuguese did not practise apartheid, it was clear the Portuguese had their own means of discrimination. A five-tier hierarchy was dominated by whites born in Portugal, followed by Angolan-born whites, then mestizos, assimilados and finally the great majority who lived far from towns, spoke tribal languages and had an average life expectancy of thirty-five years.

Despite Salazar's propaganda of a happy empire, black students from Protestant mission schools around Nova Lisboa, Angola's second largest city, had been imprisoned for joining the Organização Socialista de Angola and demanding black equality and independence. It was in this central highlands region our quixotic neighbour from rua das Chagas, Captain Henrique Galvão, had been administrator when he began his crusade against government-sponsored forced labour, euphemistically called *contractado,* contractual work. Before Galvão disappeared into a Lisbon prison he'd told the world that hundreds of thousands of Angolans were worse off than 19th-century slaves. "In those days," he said, "Negroes were personal property which the owner had an interest in keeping healthy and strong. Now a Negro is simply rented from the government, and the employer cares little if he lives or dies."

To reach Nova Lisboa, near the green centre of Angola, I travelled first to the arid south, where sea, desert and savanna meet at the port of Lobito, terminus of the British-built Benguela Railway. A new sub-tropical city built partly on sand, Lobito was surrounded by banana plantations and tempered by the Benguela current which sweeps up the coast from Antarctica. From there, the first halt on my train journey to Nova Lisboa was Benguela, port of departure for many of the three million Angolan slaves the Portuguese shipped to Brazil, but now a quiet fishing town. Then the train began a slow ascent in which gradients were as much as one in fifty.

In the vast scenic interior of big skies and cool nights, smoke

CAMINHO DE FERRO DE BENGUELA

The Benguela Railway, sole link between Central Africa and the Atlantic, was built by the British in the 1920s, destroyed by thirty years of Angolan warfare and rebuilt by the Chinese. It was the only steam railway fuelled by sweet-smelling eucalyptus wood.

from the steam engine smelt of eucalyptus from the fuel logs. At 4,000 feet we were among maize and coffee and the sisal planta-tions and the white communities of Ganda and Lepi. The climate resembled early summer in Canada and I could imagine no region in West Africa more benign, temperate and pleasant than the hills and savannas of the Angolan "Plano Alto." Along the railway, which was built in twenty-six years to transport copper from landlocked upper Congo and Rhodesia 800 miles to the port of Lobito, were the towns of Vila Nova and Silva Porto (both renamed since inde-pendence). Bié region was the bread basket of Angola, with flour mills, tile and brick factories, and cattle ranches owned by people who could never have aspired to owning land in hierarchical metropolitan Portugal. One such *quinta*, for example, was farmed by Leal Costa, a former Benguela Railway clerk, and his handsome wife and two sons. A fifth-generation Angolan, his ancestors had arrived in the 19th century; the family had never been to Portugal and their life style reminded me of early prairie Canada.

Some 5,000 feet above sea level, Nova Lisboa flourished amid orchards and maize fields whose white settlers exported grain, sugar, cotton, hides, coffee and fruit. The architecture was Portuguese; the red laterite roads, baobab trees and villages of the Umbundu people, largest ethnic group in the country, were African. Founded in 1912, Huambo's Bantu name was changed to Nova Lisboa in the 1920s when the Portuguese began the hopeful but never finished task of creating a model Angolan capital to replace 400-year-old Luanda. For Salazar, Nova Lisboa was his symbol of a revived Portuguese empire based on diamonds, coffee and oil.

Despite the dictator's insistence that Angola, Mozambique, Goa and Portugal's other colonies were basically provinces like mainland Algarve or Minho, I noticed that the white settlers I met spoke of themselves as Angolans. A few had even courted certain trouble by writing to the United Nations in New York demanding that Angola be placed under UN supervision; some blacks who had studied at Protestant missions went further and were calling for complete independence, having joined the Party of the United Struggle for Africans in Angola. Among them was the Marxist physician and poet Agostinho Neto, the man who would eventually become Angola's president after many decades of anti-colonial and civil wars. "Angola's people can liberate themselves," Neto declared, "only by revolutionary struggle that can only be won by a united front, irrespective of colour, social situation or religious belief." Salazar's carrot and stick response was to jail Neto and promise the colony development money, while sending in 3,000 troops. He strengthened the secret police and blamed Protestant missionaries for causing sedition

Canadian Protestant missions played a role in educating Angolans over the years. This is a girls' school at Cabinda, maintained by a Baptist church congregation in the Annapolis Valley village of Port Williams, Nova Scotia.

on the irrefutable grounds that all the black nationalist leaders had been trained in mission schools.

Whether Baptist, Methodist, Evangelical, Congregationalist or United Church, western missionaries had lived in Angola for generations, teaching, healing and proselytizing. In rural regions served neither by the state nor the Catholic Church, they established little schools, published tracts and Bibles in Bantu, trained local people to become pastors and explained the meaning of human equality. Some were Canadians, such as Dr. Sidney Gilchrist, a United Church medical missionary from Pictou, Nova Scotia. With his Halifax-born wife and children, Gilchrist ran a hospital, two schools, a leper clinic and sanitation projects at the central highlands mission at Dondi. Gilchrist became a critic of the government and was banned from the colony; while awaiting an opportunity to return he died in a car accident in Canada.

*   *   *

Three times as big as California, Angola was fated to become one of the most tragic of war-torn African countries but the colony in more immediate jeopardy in 1954 was the Portuguese State of India, comprising the scattered enclaves of Goa, Damão, Diu, Dadra and Nagar-Haveli strung out along the Indian west coast.

When the Portuguese captured "Golden Goa" from the Arabs in the 16th century, it was already one of the richest cities due to trade in mace, pepper and cloves from India, cinnamon from Ceylon, camphor and ivory from Africa, silk and porcelain from Cathay, frankincense and myrrh from Arabia. Celebrated by the national poet Luis de Camoens in his epic *Os Lusíadas,* which told the odyssey of Vasco da Gama, who found the sea route to the Indies, Goa four centuries later had become an anachronistic colonial outpost, half Indian, half Portuguese, with a sixty-five-mile coastline on the Arabian Sea and a population of 700,000. Apart from iron and manganese deposits it held no economic interest but immense religious and symbolic significance. In Goa rested the holy remains of St. Francis Xavier, who had lived there as a Jesuit missionary.

For decades Salazar had clung to the hope that Britain would somehow help him keep Goa by honouring a quaint 600-year-old treaty of alliance that promised "troops, archers, slingers, and galleys sufficiently armed for war." In the event, Britain refused to intervene with either archers or aircraft and in 1947 itself departed the subcontinent, whereupon Indian Prime Minister Jawaharlal Nehru tried to persuade the Portuguese to follow suit. A David and Goliath struggle began,

In 1954 a "free Goa" group based in India recruited *satyagrahis,* followers of the non-violent movement made famous half a century earlier by Mahatma Gandhi in his campaign to free India from the British. On August 15, the seventh anniversary of Britain's withdrawal and India's independence, thousands of unarmed *satyagrahis* tried to cross the Goa border but were beaten back. Throughout 1955 self-styled freedom fighters, whom the Portuguese called terrorists, attacked frontier posts under cover of darkness while by day crowds of unarmed *satyagrahis* were stopped from entering Goa by police firing over their heads. In August five thousand *satyagrahis* from Kashmir, Bengal, Punjab and Gujarat pitched tents along the forested, 160-mile border. Dressed in white and forming a human wall, they crossed the border in wave after wave, lying down when the Portuguese opened fire, rising and advancing when the guns fell silent. Twenty-two were killed, 225 injured and many imprisoned.

Nehru said it was impossible to negotiate with a government which believed in "16th century concepts of colonial conquest by force" and ordered his troops to close the border except for an entry at Polem in the southwest to allow passage of mail and travellers with passes issued in Bombay, 400 miles to the north. Nocturnal terrorist raids persisted, and though Nehru ordered the *satyagrahis* marches to cease, a demonstration was expected on Indian Independence Day in 1956. In anticipation, I flew with Portuguese journalist Dutra Faria from Lisbon to Goa on August 11, where we were met at Dabolim airport by an army major. Portuguese India was on a war footing, he said, with 12,000 troops from mainland Portugal and Mozambique.

It was monsoon season as we drove in an army jeep to the capital Panjim, twenty miles through a rainy green countryside of red earth, plantations of cashews, plantains, coconut palms, and rice paddies where buffalo stood with white birds sitting on their backs. As the darkness fell we were waiting to be ferried across the Zuari River when the jeep driver turned, and as if offering a cigarette, casually enquired if we wanted guns. The Portuguese journalist accepted a revolver and strapped it on. A gun being the last thing a journalist should be caught with, I declined.

In Panjim I booked into the new Mondovi Hotel, where novelist Evelyn Waugh had recently been a guest while attending a celebration of the life of the mummified St. Francis Xavier. That evening I had my first experience of Goa night life. Dutra and I were dining at a recommended restaurant outside the capital and though we were the only clients in the establishment, which was old and gloomy, the curry was excellent. While we were eating we became aware of soft moaning outside the open window on the dark veranda. When we paid the bill and stepped out, we found the ghostly sounds came from a long-haired girl in a sari chained to the veranda railing. The waiter came out to assure us that she was "only the owner's mad daughter."

Later that night I was having a beer in the hotel bar when a tall well-built man sat down and ordered *feni,* the powerful local brew made from fermented cashew nuts. His name, he said, was Mike, his parents were Goan but he was born in England and had served in a British anti-terrorist unit fighting communists in the jungles of Malaya. "The blighters shot me in the back – an ambush," he said, and took off his white shirt. Stitched across his broad shoulders like a blue tattoo was a neat line where he claimed automatic gunfire had grazed him. Mike, which I took to be a *nom de guerre,* said he was a mercenary working for the Portuguese government, hunting terrorists who crept into Goa at night to shoot train drivers and generally disrupt the economy. He said, "I'll take you out with us some night."

The next morning being Sunday, I attended Mass at the Church of Our Lady of Immaculate Conception, a white, 350-year-old baroque wedding cake of a building flanked by two towers and approached up a majestic flight of stone stairs. The congregation included Europeans and Goans, and after praying for peace we attended a reception and lunch given by the mayor, who told me the municipal authorities, police and judges were native Goans. Despite Indian insistence that Goans were repressed and exploited, he told me that many were reluctant to join India and believed they were better off as they were. Goan Catholics feared they would be swamped in a sea of 300 million Hindus.

After the mayor's three-hour curry lunch we went sightseeing. Although the capital, Panjim, contained temples and mosques, its churches and two-storey colonial houses in pastel yellows and blues were like those in Portugal as were the streets named rua da Natal, rua do Povo de Lisboa, each with its history. Avenida D. João de Castro commemorated a 16th-century viceroy who used his own money to feed the troops and died a pauper.

Velha Goa, eight miles up-river, was deserted, engulfed in jungle.

The seat of Portuguese power until 1759, the plague-ridden city was abandoned in favour of Panjim. There in the Basilica of Bom Jesus lay the remains of St. Francis Xavier in a silver casket, glass protecting his livid little face. At a Hindu temple pilgrims were squatting in the courtyard cooking meals and four men on a platform were beating drums to summon them to prayer. Removing our shoes, we were ushered into a great dark chamber whose only light came through slits in the stone walls, reflected by mirrors cleverly mounted outside the building on cleft sticks. A priest was giving out white paste made from ashes and cow dung which people daubed on their foreheads. I saw a statue which was part dragon and part goat. As we drove back to Panjim the monsoon rain resumed.

On August 14 Mike, as promised, took me on a night patrol. Clad in blue boiler suits, their faces smeared with burnt cork, Mike and his flying squad of ten Goan policemen drove north in the rain beyond Pernem, where the railway crosses into India, an area that had been raided by militants. All was quiet. The next day was the anniversary of India's independence and the question, said Mike, was whether the *satyagrahis* were going to heed Nehru's order to desist from suicidal marches.

August 15 dawned sunny, "a perfect day for an invasion," someone said. Standing on a road at Goa's eastern border were twelve men, police, soldiers, and journalists, and before us the green hills of the Western Ghats and a forest trail curving through the trees into the state of Maharashtra. There was no sign of *satyagrahis* or anyone else. As we stood in the hot sun at the frontier marker, speculating on who or what might lie hidden in the forest on the other side, someone suggested that as the only foreigner present – and moreover from a country which, like India, was part of the Commonwealth – I might stroll across to see what was going on.

Clutching my passport, I told them I'd be back in an hour or two and walked down the winding woodland path into India. Some ten minutes later as I rounded a bend I saw a rifle leaning against a tree and a young man washing his shirt in a stream. Startled, he ran to retrieve his gun, and since he spoke a language I did not understand I held out my passport until I realized he couldn't read and we wordlessly agreed the best thing would be for me to go with him. After a while we came to a camp where two officers were sitting in a tent at a table piled with documents. They spoke English, examined my passport and were polite, if puzzled. Didn't I know Goa was under siege? After a curry lunch during which there was some talk of putting me on a train to Bombay, they said it had been decided that since I did not have an Indian visa I must return to Goa the way I had come.

At the border late that afternoon I was greeted with relief by those who had waited since morning for me to return. With Indian troops sealing the border, a stalemate had set in. The rule of British, Spanish, Dutch and French, which had lasted for 300 years, was coming to an end and although the Portuguese India empire was 400 years old Salazar vowed it would live on and recalled that the Roman empire had lasted for a millennium.

I left Portugal to take another job in the autumn of 1956. Had I known how soon the world's oldest surviving empire would collapse I might have stayed on to witness the collapse of five centuries of Portuguese rule.

*   *   *

The scene shifts now to a snowy winter night twenty-seven years later. Boarding a Greyhound bus from Ottawa to Montreal I sat beside a dapper, middle-aged man and as we talked he said he was a military attaché at the Indian High Commission. When I mentioned my encounter with the Indian army at Goa all those years ago, he told me he had himself been in that camp though he had not been one of the officers who questioned me. He had also been in Goa six years later and described how 30,000 Indian troops with tanks and artillery captured the enclave in a day and a half although Salazar had ordered Portuguese troops to fight to the death. In the end, twenty-two Indian soldiers were killed and fifty-one wounded. Thirty Portuguese were killed and fifty-seven wounded. On December 19, 1961, Portuguese India became part of the new Indian Union and Goa, invaded by hippies, became an international tourist resort.

Angola, on the other hand, was to suffer thirty years of war. With the Soviet Union and Cuba supporting Agostinho Neto's Marxist MPLA party, and the United States and South Africa supporting Joseph Savimbi's right-wing UNITA, Angola became, like Mozambique, Vietnam, Central America and Afghanistan, a Cold War proxy. Angola won independence under President Neto in 1975, but millions died in the fight for independence and the civil war that followed. Much of the country's infrastructure was destroyed in a war from which it is still recovering amid portents of a new colonialism. The Portuguese Benguela Railway, built by the British, is being rebuilt by China, which, in Angola as in Mozambique, is, I hear, showing the arrogant attitudes of a new imperialism.

10

A HOT AND COLD WAR

At a chance meeting in 1956 with a former colleague at a Lisbon garden party I was offered employment in that grey area between uneasy peace and nuclear holocaust called the Cold War.

Talbot Hood and I had worked the night shift together at United Press in London in 1951 but had lost touch and I had not seen him until that Fourth of July party in the American Embassy garden. Now an executive with Radio Free Europe (RFE) in Munich, Talbot might be mistaken for an Englishman, one of those quiet, moustached, anglicized Americans who marry British women and carry a rolled umbrella. Having explained he was in Lisbon to inspect the transmitter RFE had built, the better to bounce medium-wave transmissions off the upper atmosphere into East Europe, Hood mentioned RFE was recruiting for its news team in Munich. Although his offer would have tripled my salary and provided free housing, I was at the time awaiting a promised United Press transfer and looking forward to living in London again. Tal told me to let him know if I changed my mind.

Communist Europe was much in the news that summer. Nikita Khrushchev's denunciation of Stalin's reign of terror, supposedly a secret speech to the 20th Soviet Party Congress, had been leaked to the west and broadcast by Radio Free Europe. In response, workers in the Polish industrial city of Poznan staged a massive strike protesting ten years of Stalinist occupation. Shouting "bread and freedom," they blocked roads, freed political prisoners, shut railway stations and smashed equipment used to jam foreign broadcasts.

By early autumn the Polish government was promising reforms

known as "the Polish thaw" and the turmoil had spread to Hungary, whose leader Matyas "Little Stalin" Rákosi had jailed, exiled or murdered politicians, priests and labour leaders, eliminated unions, seized private property and reduced schools and media to puppets. Early in October, my transfer to UP London having been indefinitely postponed and finding Lisbon a dead end, I flew to Munich and accepted Talbot Hood's offer.

Located in its own modern building in the Englischer Garten, Munich's biggest park, Radio Free Europe had been broadcasting since 1952 in Hungarian, Polish, Czech, Slovak and Romanian. Elsewhere in Munich RFE's American-sponsored twin, Radio Liberty, was broadcasting to the Soviet Union. With a budget of $21 million, which we later discovered was channelled covertly through the CIA before Congress took over the financing directly, RFE's mandate was to agitate for change. RFE's one thousand employees included émigrés whose political beliefs ranged from extreme right to moderate left and according to the RFE handbook they were admonished to "remind listeners constantly they are governed by agents of a foreign power whose purpose is not to further national interest but the interest of the Soviet Union."

RFE's American staff included academics in a Political Advisor's Office headed by William E. ("Bill") Griffith, a clever young political scientist from Harvard and later a professor at Massachusetts Institute of Technology and sometime associate of Canadian-born Washington foreign policy guru Zbigniew Brzezinski. In three years Griffith had made RFE an international centre for serious Communist studies which attracted scholars from Europe and America. Although the CIA used RFE as one of its sources of information, so far as I could tell it had little influence on the policies of the organization.

In its efforts to break the communists' monopoly on information, RFE's round-the-clock news, commentary, plays, music (including rock and roll) and religion was the sort of programming listeners might expect if their radios were free of communist indoctrination. Hourly newscasts were compiled from information supplied through the central newsroom, from Associated Press, United Press, Reuters and Agence France Presse as well as RFE staff correspondents, mostly mainstream newsmen based in London, Paris, Rome, Athens, Vienna, Brussels, Berlin, New York and Washington.

In early October I was still in Lisbon with Margaret and the children awaiting my UP replacement to arrive when the Hungarian Revolution began. Inspired by the Poles, Budapest university students demanded multi-party elections, a free press, the right to strike, dismissal of the AVH secret police and withdrawal of the Soviet troops based in Hungary under the Warsaw Pact. They also demanded the return of deposed Prime Minister Imre Nagy.

The crisis came on the chilly, foggy evening of Tuesday, October 23, when a massive crowd of citizens marched to Parliament Square in Budapest. "At the head of our column were flags," recalled a marcher. "An old woman waving a pair of scissors reached up, grabbed a flag and cut the Red star out of the centre. It was a tremendous moment." The speeches and patriotic songs were peaceful until the despised Stalinist Erno Gero, who had been Rákosi's deputy, went on the air at Radio Budapest and called the demonstrators "a reactionary mob." The crowd reacted all right – by toppling a statue of Stalin, shouting *"Ruszkik haza!"* ("Russians go home!"), and marching to the radio station, joined by trucks of armed workers from the industrial suburbs. When the green-uniformed AVH security police opened fire, killing several people, fighting spread through the city. That night an alarmed government chose the moderate Imre Nagy to replace Gero, who had invited the Soviet army to restore order. At 2 a.m. Soviet tanks rolled into the capital.

When tank commanders in Parliament Square turned their guns on the crowd, fighting escalated through the narrow streets and into the countryside, with Freedom Fighters attacking Soviet tanks with rifles, cobblestones and Molotov cocktails, the homemade fire bombs named for the Soviet foreign minister. Bodies lay in the streets beside charred tanks. Nagy appealed for a ceasefire and promised "extended democratization" and dissolution of the AVH, the only organization still supporting Soviet rule, and declared foreign broadcasts no longer illegal. In an unusual gesture of reconciliation, Moscow issued a statement which regretted the bloodshed, admitted "errors and violations" and concluded that "the Soviet government is ready to begin negotiations on the question of Soviet troops on Hungarian territory."

On All Soul's Day, November 1, the tenth day of the Hungarian Revolution, I flew to Munich with Margaret, Marina and Karen to become chief of RFE's central newsroom. The news that evening was encouraging. A ceasefire had been declared, the Soviet army had withdrawn from Budapest, leaving the mangled streets to Freedom Fighters and the Hungarian army. "We Salute the Glorious Dawn," proclaimed the communist newspaper *Szabad Nep*. There was talk of democracy, perhaps another Austria or Finland.

Margaret and I spent the cold, rainy weekend moving into a top-floor apartment at 230 Arcisstrasse, a pale yellow stucco block in downtown Munich which housed RFE families of several nationalities. Having been in Germany in the spring of 1945 when all had been destruction, gloom and defiance, I now found a friendly Americanized nation rising out of the rubble. We dined Saturday evening in a *Weinstube* amid happy, well-fed Bavarians and awoke Sunday morning to one of the darkest, bloodiest days of the Cold War.

At 4:15 a.m. the Red Army launched a massive attack – eight divisions, tanks, artillery, planes – which was resisted by a guerilla force of workers, students and Hungarian soldiers armed with rifles and Molotov cocktails. At dawn, the voice of Prime Minister Imre Nagy calling for help was heard on radio for the last time.

"We were awakened by heavy guns bombarding the city," recalled journalist George Horvath. "Freedom Fighters were trapped in barracks and blocks of flats. The Russians bombarded every house from which a single shot was fired. This senseless Russian massacre provoked armed resistance, bitter fighting and a general strike." The death toll would mount to an estimated 2,500 Hungarians and 700 Russians.

When I reported for work in Munich Monday morning, fighting was still raging through Hungary, as it would for another week, and the RFE building had the feel of a hospital the morning after a disaster. Voices were muted, people pale and distressed. Refugees fleeing through the rain and sleet into Austria in their tens of thousands, bound eventually for Canada, Britain, the United States and Australia, brought disturbing accusations that RFE's Hungarian Service had made things worse during the rebellion by broadcasting empty promises of American military help. Since the United States, despite its rhetoric, had no intention of risking atomic war, RFE would have been wiser telling Hungarians the only aid was to be food and medicine.

In the investigations that followed it was found that whereas RFE had stressed restraint and "liberalization" during the earlier Polish crisis, RFE's Hungarian service, called the Voice of Free Hungary, had repeatedly violated internal directives by references to possible armed western assistance and broadcasting advice on how to sabotage telephone and railway lines. The most notable lapse was a press review which followed the noon news bulletin on Sunday, November 4. "If the Hungarians hold out for three or four days, pressure on the United States to send military help to the Freedom Fighters will become irresistible," the Washington correspondent of the London *Observer* had written. "If the Hungarians can continue to fight until Wednesday we shall be closer to a world war than at any time since 1939." The Voice of Free Hungary, relaying this comment to

Broadcasting to five countries, Radio Free Europe at its best provided a window on the West and an alternative to the virtual Communist monopoly on information.

listeners, added, "In the Western capitals a practical manifestation of Western sympathy is expected at any hour."

Words that might seem anodyne in London were dangerous on the streets of Budapest. In the reorganization which followed, right-wing "cold war warriors" were replaced by young émigrés who had more recent experience in Hungary. Throughout RFE there was a more balanced, professional approach, less insistence on "American values" and more programming explaining Western Europe to Eastern Europe.

I had found RFE's central newsroom more of a sorting station than an editorial function, tucked away in the basement and suffering from a lack of status. News pouring in on high-speed wire-service teletypes ran immediately into a bottleneck as it was processed

The RFE central newsroom in Munich was staffed around the clock by Americans, Canadians, British and Australians. World news was channelled to the separate language services to be tailored and translated for each country.

through mimeograph machines and deposited in pigeon holes for hand delivery around the building, a slow, old-fashioned system that made editing difficult. Reports from RFE correspondents which should have been telexed were laboriously transcribed off the phone when an editor could find the time. Apart from my predecessor, who had been editor of a major American daily newspaper, the staff of young American expatriates had little journalistic experience.

My first task was to find a large enough space on the ground floor to convert into a newsroom with a traditional u-shaped copy desk. We then connected to our customers, the various language sections around the building, by an internal teletype line, which gave us speed and the opportunity to compare and edit incoming news.

We hired several professional British and Australian journalists, men who saw RFE as a job rather than a crusade. I then spent a week at Bush House in London observing the Overseas Service of the BBC, which in twenty years had built an unrivalled reputation for credibility. There 240 people churned out 200 news bulletins every twenty-four hours in forty languages. "Giving the news factually, means we take great care to avoid comment," said a Bush House manual. "The objectivity of bulletins wins listeners, particularly in countries where news is controlled and censored." After stressing accuracy, balance and objectivity, it warned against loaded language: adjectives ("the heroic defenders") that suggested partisanship, verbs like "refute" or "claim" (rather than "deny" or "say") and belittling adverbs ("The opposition gained only five seats"). The Overseas Service was impressive, bureaucratic and, being English, consumed gallons of strong tea and piles of sweet buns. The "duty editor" in what one staffer aptly called a "news factory" controlled each item until it was broadcast, but at RFE we decided to leave editorial responsibility with each language desk, a system the BBC itself later emulated in its East Europe service.

*   *   *

My three years in Munich were rewarding. Despite the wartime bombing, the city centre – Marienplatz, Frauenkirche, the Rathaus-Glockenspiel and Schwabing, the Bohemian quarter – retained its medieval charm. There were masked balls during the Lenten carnival of Fasching, concerts, opera, and the Alte Pinakothek for art, the Hofbräuhaus and Oktoberfest for beer. In the city that gave Hitler his start, no one spoke of the war. With the Alps beckoning on the horizon, Margaret and I skied in winter and climbed in summer. My most memorable climb was on the 2,628-metre Alpspitze, which I unwisely tackled alone one September Saturday, writing my name in the book in the tin box under the cross, and came home exhausted.

Munich was wonderfully situated for train travel – to Venice, Vienna, Rome, the coast of Croatia, Greece and Berlin. The children were starting school and speaking German. It was a good life, but at age thirty-four I had saved enough money to try my hand at something I had long wanted to do – free-lancing in London. I felt that life at RFE was becoming too predictable, but in this I was wrong for the Soviet empire was soon to attack RFE with deadly effect.

Marina (right) and Karen in Munich.

The anti-RFE campaign began with attempts by the Polish secret service to subvert RFE staff and infiltrate agents. Then Czechoslovaks joined in. A few months after I left Munich the salt shakers were poisoned in RFE's basement cafeteria, which I had daily frequented for knackwurst, weisswurst, leberkäs and dunkles beer. Bizarrely, a Czech consular official based in Salzburg had entrusted the deed to a double agent, who played both sides and informed RFE before any damage was done. The salt shakers contained atropine, a white, crystalline alkaloid poison derived from deadly nightshade.

By 1976 RFE's enemies were resorting to assassination. Emil Georgescu, a Romanian government lawyer who'd defected to work for RFE, suffered a mysterious knife attack. Two years later Georgi Markov, author and political commentator who had ignored warnings to cease attacks on Todor Zhivkov, Bulgaria's dictator, was waiting for a bus near Waterloo Bridge in London when he felt a pain in his leg. Markov had been stabbed with an umbrella tipped with ricin, a lethal derivative of castor oil seeds for which there was no antidote. The assailant escaped in the confusion and Markov died three days later.

Then it was the turn of the Romanians. At 9:47 p.m. on Saturday, February 21, 1981, they struck with a fifteen-kilo plastic explosive which destroyed part of the RFE building in Munich and injured several people, although the assassin had thoughtfully chosen a Saturday evening when few were on duty. The attack was planned by the professional terrorist Carlos the Jackal at the instructions of the Romanian dictator, Nicolae Ceausescu.

Ten months later, on December 21, 1981, I heard that my friend Noel Bernard, head of RFE's Romanian service, had died of "virulent cancer." Born in Romania of a Jewish father and Catholic mother, Noel was my age, an apparently healthy fifty-six, with whom I had worked and played tennis in Munich and London. I'd first met Noel in 1956 and our careers had coincided after we both left RFE to take jobs in London broadcasting to the United States. When United Press, where I was again working, bought out Noel's organization, he returned to Munich, where his clever attacks on the despotic President Ceausescu drew a large Romanian audience. After Noel's death there were inevitable rumours of foul play when Noel's successor, Vlad Georgescu, also died of cancer after receiving warnings. It

RFE's Noel Bernard was allegedly poisoned on the orders of Nicolae Ceausescu, president of Communist Romania. On December 18, 2005, two decades after Bernard's death, President Trian Basescu paid tribute in the post-Communist parliament to Bernard and Vlad Georgescu, "men who fought selflessly and passionately for the truth and to make it known."

seemed for many years that the questions surrounding Noel's death would remain unanswered.

The Cold War had been over for twenty years and the communist regimes long gone when Romania's intelligence service revealed a 1980 government dossier which stated Noel Bernard had indeed been targeted. With post-Cold-War secrets now falling out of the Soviet closet, it became known that the Soviet KGB and its counterpart in Romania had used a radioactive weapon they called radu, which led to conjecture the RFE deaths had been caused by radioactive thallium powder which, placed in a victim's food, produced effects that emulated cancer. Although FBI investigations failed to find supporting evidence, a defector to the United States, a former Romanian *Securitate* chief and Ceausescu advisor, then came forward. In an article in the American *National Review* in November 2006, Lieutenant General Ion Mihai Pacepa wrote that while on a hunting trip with Ceausescu, he heard the president of Romania demand that Noel Bernard be given radiation poisoning. "On the unforgettable day of July 22, 1978," Pacepa wrote, "Ceausescu and I were hiding inside a pelican blind in a remote corner of the Danube Delta, where not even a passing bird could overhear us. 'I want you to give radu to Noel Bernard,' Ceausescu whispered into my ear. 'You don't need to report back to me on the results, I'll learn (about) them from Western newspapers....'"

11

THE WORLD TURNED
UPSIDE DOWN

"If summer were spring and the other way round,
Then all the world would turn upside down."
17th century London ballad.

London in the gloriously sunny summer of 1959 was rejuvenated and affluent. The Conservative government called it the New Elizabethan Age, for Britain was booming like the rest of Europe with postwar reconstruction. Gone were the gritty austerities and the killer smog that killed 4,000 Londoners in 1952.

Cars and tourists had not yet overpowered the West End, so London was easy to get around. For the first few months I lived with American friends in an 18th-century house on Chelsea's Cheyne Walk, a street that was home at various times to George Eliot, Dante Gabriel Rossetti, David Lloyd George, Mick Jagger and Marianne Faithfull. I'd moved on before Michelangelo Antonioni arrived at number 100 to shoot the three-day party for his movie *Blow Up*.

House hunting being a good way to get to know a city, one hot and humid August afternoon I walked from the Thames Embankment to a brownstone mansion in the Boltons in South Kensington where a fifth-floor flat was renting for an unbelievable £125 a year. It was an odd place. I opened the door and entered directly into a huge chamber that had been the ballroom of a grand town house before it was butchered into flats. With floor-to-ceiling windows looking south toward Crystal Palace, the room took up 80 per cent of the flat; the rest consisting of two small bedrooms and a pantry with a cold-water tap but no kitchen. The previous tenants, I was told, had been an old couple, one or both of whom had died of smoke inhalation. A charred mattress told the sad tale. I was about ready to rent this monstrosity until I stepped back out into the hall, pulled open the heavy wrought-iron elevator door, and clutched the door frame to keep from falling five floors to the basement. A 19th-century elevator was no place for two small daughters.

Chelsea had retained a village charm, but my favourite area was Hampstead. On those airy northern heights I found a flat renting for £10 a week at 14 Lyndhurst Gardens near Belsize Park Station on the Northern Line and not far from Hampstead Heath and Booklovers Corner, where George Orwell once worked. Recently occupied by Max Wall, the comedian who invented the funny walk perfected a generation later by John Cleese, our new home was the ground floor of a three-storey, red-brick Victorian mansion once called Tynehome. Built in the 1880s when Hampstead was rural, the house had originally had "a noble dining room," "an elegant drawing room," a basement kitchen with rooms for servants, and tennis and croquet lawns in the garden.

Since the 1930s the house had been cut into four flats, one on each level, but retained hardwood floors, tall windows, rare central heating, fireplace and neglected garden. I painted the faded walls in delft blue and oyster shell white and waited for Margaret, who was at her parents' home in Toronto recovering from a broken leg suffered in an Austrian skiing accident, to come with Marina, aged five, and Karen, three. Marina, Karen, our black cat Jackie and I would live at Lyndhurst Gardens for ten years, Margaret for only four.

The winds of change were already blowing London into the Swinging Sixties. The most obvious change had been the immigration from Britain's colonies in the West Indies, Africa and India. Primarily meant to redress a postwar labour shortage, immigration was creating a truly multiracial and multicultural city. The prim BBC, no longer the sole social arbiter, was losing its national monopoly and having to learn to compete with brash new commercial media, including offshore pirate radio stations. A relaxation of cultural censorship encouraged self-styled Angry Young Men to satirize authority to a degree unseen since the 18th century. Our neighbour David Storey, a novelist and playwright from Yorkshire, was writing about northern working class life and, along with John Osborne's seminal *Look Back In Anger* at the Royal Court and Arnold Wesker's *The Kitchen,* his plays were transforming British theatre.

The Conservative government, more or less acquiescent in Labour's welfare state if not in a classless society, passed an act encouraging the working class to attend university. Having proclaimed class war obsolete while attacking the "doctrinaire nightmare of socialism and nationalism," the upper class Prime Minister Harold Macmillan was on firmer ground when he assured the nation that "Most of our people have never had it so good."

People were buying consumer goods they'd only dreamed of: televisions, washing machines, vacuum cleaners, refrigerators, and small cars to replace their bicycles and sidecar motorcycles. Glossy magazines, commercial TV and Hollywood movies had given the British a craving for American materialism. Jack Cohen opened Tesco, Britain's first self-service supermarket, in an abandoned suburban cinema, and changed High Street shopping forever. Youngsters in Edwardian frock coats or leather jackets created new markets for music, clothes and recreational drugs.

In September 1959 I set up shop as a freelance working out of a little studio on Wardour Street in Soho, my first assignment being a CBC radio documentary on the wartime revolt in the Warsaw Ghetto. Survivors of the 1943 uprising living in Tel Aviv, Toronto and New York were prepared to tell their stories and my own assignment was to fly to Warsaw on LOT, the Polish airline, to view the place where 20,000 Jews were killed fighting their Nazi oppressors.

Having so recently worked at anti-communist Radio Free Europe, I expected trouble getting a visa but there was none.

As a taxi took me into Warsaw from the airport I saw much war damage. The driver told me the crowded cafés were not evidence of affluence but of a severe housing shortage; there were queues for black bread and sausage. The suburbs were pocked with bullet and shell holes but the city centre was a surprise. Instead of heaps of rubble, 16th-century buildings had been restored to the smallest architectural details. Spoiling the effect was the ugly new Palace of Arts and Culture, a gift from Moscow.

On Anielewicza and Zamenhofa streets, where the ghetto had flourished, there were guides who showed me around the ruins and the Gestapo building where bullet holes in cell walls told their chilling story. As the survivors had related, in the spring of 1943 the elders realized the Nazis had been lying and the trains supposedly transporting Jews to "resettlement camps" were taking them to be murdered in the gas chambers of Treblinka, and on April 19, 1943, the Jews decided to fight for their lives. On the fifth day of the uprising the Nazis began to destroy the ghetto block by block but the people resisted for an heroic twenty-eight days, fighting from cellars and sewers. In addition to those killed in the fighting, 36,000 were sent to the gas chambers. An estimated 300 SS troops were killed and 1,000 wounded.

Back in London I worked on assignments for the Overseas Service of the BBC, the Canadian Broadcasting Corporation, the Voice of America, Radio Free Europe, Westinghouse Broadcasting and the Mutual Broadcasting System in the United States, assignments which ranged from interviews with newsmakers to coverage of a dam collapse that killed 400 people in Fréjus in southern France and an earthquake at Agadir, Morocco, that killed 12,000. When there was no hard news I tapped the market for the eccentric British anachronisms beloved by Americans: the 13th-century Ceremony of

On the last of the sailing barges to scud up the Thames Estuary, Bob Roberts sang sea songs and ran his little ship with only the aid of a small dog he taught to climb the mast like a monkey – or a proper sailor.

the Keys, where Yeomen of the Guard in ancient uniforms marched with a drummer each evening to lock the Tower of London with the Queen's Keys; or the 600-year-old annual Trial of the Pyx, a box of newly minted coins which a judge and jury inspected for flaws; the World Conkers Championship in the village of Ashton; the World Custard Pie Throwing Championships in Kent; and the old woman in Hastings who lived not in a shoe but in a yellow house shaped like a cheddar cheese.

Down on the Thames I interviewed Bob Roberts, the last cloth-cap skipper still navigating freight sailing barges between York-shire and London in fair weather and foul. There had once been two thousand barges and their billowing red-brown sails scudding through the Thames estuary had been a stirring sight for centuries. Now there was only Bob's wooden *Cambria*, 92 feet long, 100 tons, no engine but the wind. Bob's sole crew member was a little sea dog (a lurcher, prized by poachers), which he had taught to shinny up the mast like a monkey. Bob played an accordion and sang "The Bold Princess Royal," a song about a tall ship which outwitted pi-rates on the banks off Newfoundland.

I learned to tread warily when interviewing the famous. During an interview with ninety-year-old Lord Bertrand Russell at his home in Wales my unwieldy green box of a 1950s BBC tape recorder broke down and the great philosopher and humanist complained I'd caused him to lose his train of thought; luckily it happened near the end of our session so I had something to take back to the BBC. On another occasion, arriving early for an interview with the biologist and UNESCO Director General Sir Julian Huxley, I followed the directions of the new maid at Huxley's home in Keats Grove, Hampstead, walked upstairs and gently knocked on the door indicated. The door creaked open to reveal the elder brother of novelist Aldous and grandson of the great Victorian educator T.H. Huxley struggling to get into his trousers. We were off on the wrong foot, so to speak. Sir Julian evidently didn't suffer fools, but once his annoyance dissipated he offered coffee and related his distress at the environmental destruction he had recently found in East Africa – too many animals being hunted, too much natural habitat destroyed. He gave me a preview of his plan for an international, non-governmental, scientific and technical solution to save the natural world. The following year, with the Duke of Edinburgh, Huxley created the World Wildlife Fund, based in Switzerland, one of most important non-governmental organizations concerned with the global environment.

One mild evening in October I took the train to see Winston Churchill at Woodford on the northeastern outskirts of London, as I had eight years earlier during his 1951 election campaign. The old man had suffered another stroke at the age of eighty but was running for election, a chequered lifetime after gaining fame as a brash young war correspondent. Elected to parliament at twenty-five, at thirty-two a controversial Home Secretary advocating social reform, he was First Lord of the Admiralty in World War I when he was blamed for the slaughter at Gallipoli.

On that October night in 1959 in Woodford, the man who had

Still hale in this wartime Ottawa photo, Churchill suffered a series of strokes in the 1950s. After a fall in 1962 his health sharply deteriorated although he remained a Member of Parliament until a month before his ninetieth birthday in 1964.

found his destiny as John Bull incarnate during World War II, spoke to a small crowd of supporters not of his tumultuous past but of the unknown future, and of his conversion to the belief that only world government could avert another world war. "The leading men of various nations," he said, "should be able to meet together, without trying to cut attitudes before excitable publics ... let us see if there is not something better for all than tearing and blasting each other to pieces." Churchill, frail and forgetful, won his seat in the general election that, coincidentally, was the political debut of young Margaret Thatcher.

Freelancing was irregular, and with a family to support I acquired a steadier income more by happenstance than design. Up to the 1960s only the major American networks, such as Edward R. Murrow's CBS, could afford daily transatlantic broadcasts from London. Now, however, the proliferation of transatlantic cable channels had lowered the cost so much that smaller outfits could afford them. Newsmen with radio experience and North American accents being few in Britain, I was offered a job as correspondent for the RKO radio network, which had stations throughout the U.S. and whose flagship was WOR, New York.

My first assignment was the wedding of Princess Margaret to Antony Armstrong-Jones on May 6, 1960. On that sunny spring morning the twenty-nine-year-old princess arrived at Westminster Abbey in a glass coach, accompanied by her brother-in-law, Prince Philip, and cheered by thousands in the streets and admired by two thousand in the Abbey. Being the same age as the Queen, I remembered when the bride was "Lilebet's" little sister, the winsome Margaret Rose, who grew to become the brainy, restless young society woman with a wicked sense of humour. Denied the love of her life, divorced Group Captain Peter Townsend, by the church, the State and her family, she now was proceeding demurely up the blue-carpeted aisle, a diminutive figure in white silk and diamond tiara, to marry the thirty-year-old society photographer she had met at a Chelsea party. It was the first televised royal wedding and was watched by twenty million viewers. That she was to suffer from ill health and a somewhat bohemian life style in later years seemed impossible on that sunny spring morning. As HRH The Princess Margaret, Countess of Snowdon, Margaret gave birth to a boy and a girl but after eighteen years and rumours of extramarital affairs the marriage ended in a troubled divorce. In those days the media were more circumspect with royalty but even so the Snowdons' social life, which included trendy people of Tony's circle, became the subject of gossip which grew until her untimely death at the age of seventy-one. Like her father, she had been a heavy smoker and suffered years of serious illnesses.

A week after the royal wedding I flew to Paris, where Russia, the United States, Britain and France, in the persons of Nikita Khrushchev, Dwight D. Eisenhower, Harold Macmillan and Charles de Gaulle, were to meet in the freshly scrubbed salon of the Élysée Palace where Madame de Pompadour had held court. A thaw in the Cold War was anticipated; if anyone could break the ice it might be the smart clownish Nikita. So when that unpredictable Russian bear stood up at a press conference at noon on May 16 he had our full attention as he ferociously accused the United States of treacherous aggression for sending a U-2 spy plane over Russia. The plane had ignominiously been shot down and the pilot, Captain Gary Powers, imprisoned, so the Americans could hardly disown the incident as they wished to do. Khrushchev made the most of the debacle, demanding an apology, which the embarrassed Eisenhower refused to provide. The Big Four Summit, toward which the superpowers had been inching, collapsed three hours after it began. Although this had seemed disastrous at the time, despite some near misses the most dangerous years of the Cold War were to pass without a major explosion. Despite the rhetoric from Washington and Moscow and episodes like the Hungarian Revolution and the Cuban missile crisis to remind us that nuclear war was always possible, the Cold War was waged through propaganda, espionage, proxy colonial conflicts and economic and technological competition..

One of the most dangerous spots was Berlin the following summer. A vulnerable link in the Iron Curtain a hundred miles inside the Soviet Occupation Zone, West Berlin was controlled by the Americans and a magnet for citizens of the German Democratic Republic (GDR), who were fleeing Soviet-style communism at the rate of four thousand a week. Khrushchev was obviously testing the new American president, Jack Kennedy, by demanding the whole city join East Germany. After Kennedy refused, on Sunday August 13, 1961, the communists split greater Berlin with a fence of mesh and barbed wire which they insisted was a barricade to keep out spies. Having strung twenty-seven miles of wire, they then built an *"anti-faschistischer Schutzwall"* or "anti-fascist wall" with concrete blocks. Streets were torn up and buildings evacuated and demolished to create a "death zone" of booby traps and trip wires. Border guards were instructed to shoot escapees on sight, the first fatality being an eighteen-year-old apprentice brick layer shot in the back while running toward freedom. It was the first of scores of such deaths.

I flew into Tempelhof airport from London on August 23 to begin nightly broadcasts to the United States. East Germans were being killed or injured every day while leaping over the wall or tunnelling from basements and graveyards. An East German border guard defected by leaping over the barbed wire, clutching his rifle. One afternoon noisy crowds gathered near Friedrichstrasse and Checkpoint Charlie, which had been set up to allow foreigners to cross. It was a pleasant Sunday and most people had come to wave across the barrier at friends and relatives, but on the West Berlin side some had come to jeer at GDR border guards and the workmen converting the wire fence into a cement wall. When West Berliners began lobbing stones at a sound truck blaring communist slogans, a GDR water canon truck popped out of a side street. The afternoon was turning ugly until American soldiers coaxed angry, frustrated West Berliners out of harm's way.

Although the Germans were segregated, by simply taking the S-bahn train in West Berlin for the short trip to Marx-Engels Platz, foreigners including us reporters could visit East Berlin as tourists. There was not much to see: grey buildings, shoddy clothes, harassed people, Soviet tanks, drab shops and eating establishment with little to sell. To learn Russian intentions the Americans risked sending an armed convoy to West Berlin along the autobahns of East Germany, and when the convoy reached beleaguered West Berlin without being challenged it became clear the communists wished to avoid a shooting war. Nearly thirty years would pass before the ugly monument to a harsh political system was torn down. Before its demise, the wall was twelve feet high and encompassed 200 streets. The death toll had reached one hundred.

That September a new crisis began after the Russians broke a year-long truce and tested a hydrogen bomb. In protest, thousands joined the Campaign for Nuclear Disarmament (CND) in a series of demonstrations against British and U.S. nuclear policies as well as those of Russia. Lord Bertrand Russell, philosopher, mathematician and Nobel Prize winner, was arrested and charged in Bow Street Magistrates Court with inciting civil disobedience. When the judge asked if he were "willing to be bound over to be of good behaviour and keep the peace," the old philosopher shouted "No" and was sen-

The March 1962 disarmament conference in Geneva was one of the series of negotiations on control of nuclear weapons that led to a 1963 nuclear test ban treaty.

....

RADIO   № 2126

Nom : ....MAC KAY.............

Prénom : ....William Donald..........

Représentant :
.....WOR.....

Nationalité:
..........Canada..........

Chargé de l'accréditation

DÉSARMEMENT   Correspondant
Genève, Mars 1962   Technicien - Assistant
                                    T.s.v.p.

tenced to a month in Brixton Prison, where he had spent six months as a conscientious objector during World War I.

Freed after a week this time, Russell agreed to a taped interview at his home, Plas Penrhyn, north Wales, a Regency house overlooking the sea near Mount Snowdon. I was shown in by his attractive fourth wife, sixty-one-year-old American academic Edith Finch, and although I had seen Lord Russell at London ban-the-bomb demonstrations and Aldermaston marches, I had never sat down with him before.

At ninety, Russell was wearing a suit with vest and a watch chain and seemed deaf and fragile. He had been ill but continued writing and lecturing and smoking the pipe tobacco he'd enjoyed for seventy years. I could see why a friend had written that his long white hair and thin face reminded one of Sir John Tenniel's Mad Hatter in *Alice in Wonderland.*

Having agreed to our interview to publicize the Bertrand Russell Peace Foundation, he said he had no intention of renouncing civil disobedience or his demands for unilateral disarmament but was aware that even multilateral disarmament was not the answer. Like Churchill, with whom he disagreed on other matters, he thought the answer lay in effective world government. He lived long enough to see a partial test ban treaty signed but not the end of the Cold War.

Early in 1962, United Press asked me to head the overseas section of a new broadcast service. Now called United Press International, the agency employed 10,000 people around the world and was distributing news in print, pictures, TV and radio to 5,400 clients in seventy countries. Having worked for UP from 1945 to 1956, I was rejoining a sort of family. Sadly, at that time I was losing my partner in my real family in what were to be the most confusing and painful months of my life. After seventeen years of a marriage which had been all I could have wished, Margaret at the age of forty was going through a crisis. We tried professional help to no avail. Whatever was happening, it led in 1963 to her leaving and to our divorce. For me the world turned upside down in the general upheaval of the Swinging Sixties. We remained friends and by mutual agreement Marina and Karen stayed with me at Lyndhurst Gardens, and Margaret came to visit them on weekends. I hired an elderly housekeeper, thankful my job was London-based. When Reuters offered me the post of South American correspondent based in Rio de Janeiro, I decided it would entail too much travel away from the children and opted to remain at UPI in London.

As I write this forty years later, divorces are much more common than they were then and an attempt to explain how and why this particular marriage failed would take chapters, even a book, and still probably wouldn't get it right. Margaret died of cancer in 1991 and I helped arrange for the memorial service and her resting place. About all I can say now is that Margaret had enhanced my life in the years we were together and that the 1960s were a time when cultural conventions which had seemed enduring were swiftly changing, and vibrant women no longer felt constrained by Victorian ideals.

*   *   *

In tune with changing times, the news that damaged Harold Macmillan's Conservative government during the long, hard winter of 1963 was no great affair of state but a cabinet minister's affair with a pretty young call girl. There had been a time when illicit sex in high places had been routinely hushed up on Fleet Street, but not during the Cold War when the official was John Profumo, wealthy Minister of State for War married to a movie star, and not when his paramour, Christine Keeler, was concurrently sleeping with the naval attaché from the Soviet Union. Having lied about the affair in Parliament, Profumo resigned, as did Macmillan some months later, by which time Winston Churchill, who had retired as prime minister in 1955, was back in the news, having rarely left it.

For years Churchill had been prone to strokes, though when they occurred we were usually told he was simply "suffering from exhaustion." Sometimes they were false alarms, as in 1960 when he was

At the height of the Cold War in 1963, Harold Macmillan's Conservative government was rocked when his Minister of State for War, John Profumo, resigned and confessed he had lied to the House of Commons about his relationship with the call girl friend of a Russian military attaché. Profumo spent the rest of his life dedicated to charity work in London's East End.

vacationing at the Hotel de Paris in Monte Carlo as the guest of Aristotle Onassis, and a reporter, hearing Churchill had had a stroke, found him dining at the Riviera home of his old government colleague Lord Beaverbrook. There was another alarm in the spring of 1962 when Churchill, again at Monte Carlo, fell and broke his thigh. That, too, he survived, but in 1964 reports began to circulate that Churchill was seriously ill. He had resigned his seat and was rarely seen in public. On his ninetieth birthday in November we saw his tired wave from a window in his Hyde Park Gate home, where he sat for hours slumped in his chair before the fire, neither reading nor speaking. Three months later, at eight-thirty on a cold wet January morning, we were summoned to hear a spokesman at Hyde Park Gate tell us, "Sir Winston died in peace and without pain." He had suffered a massive stroke from which he never regained consciousness.

The funeral six days later was the grandest state funeral granted a commoner: the tolling of Big Tom in St. Paul's Cathedral, the dirge of military bands, the singing of "To Be a Pilgrim," the insistent nineteen-gun salute echoing through the City, all the Victorian magnificence. As the cortege slow-marched to the funeral barge on the Thames on that damp freezing day, massed Highland pipes played a lament. As the barge moved up-river, the huge industrial cranes along the banks of the Thames were synchronized to bow down as the barge passed on its journey toward his resting place in a grave near Blenheim Palace, where he was born in 1874, the son of Lord Randolph Churchill and American-born Jennie Jerome. Churchill had served under six monarchs – Queen Victoria, Edward VII, George V, Edward VIII, George VI and Queen Elizabeth II. This surely was an historic time when a man's death truly marked the end of an age.

12

THE SWINGING SIXTIES

Beatlemania, the Rolling Stones, the Who, psychedelic art, Carnaby Street, drugs, miniskirts, mods and rockers, pirate radio. It is difficult now to remember when it all began, but one memorable date was surely the November day in 1955 when a twenty-one-year-old London art student began creating unique fashions in her shop on the King's Road in Chelsea. Diana Melly, who worked there, recently recalled: "At Mary Quant's Bazaar there was a sense of the new and exciting, of being in the forefront of change, and of course we were always being written about in the papers."

Young people from London's East End and the mill towns of the north were breaking cultural and social barriers that had been entrenched for centuries. The golden boys and girls in the West End were no longer the idle rich of Evelyn Waugh's Mayfair but hardworking actors Michael Caine, Rita Tushingham, Peter O'Toole and Albert Finney and playwrights Arnold Wesker, Harold Pinter, Shelagh Delaney and our Hampstead neighbour David Storey. The genteel plays of Noel Coward and Terence Rattigan were passé, an upper-class accent no longer necessary for success. At Eton a bewildered master of England's premier private school complained that his upper-crust students were talking like Cockneys. "Suddenly everyone wants to be like us," said actor Terence Stamp, son of a Thames tugboat skipper.

The biggest change, overnight it seemed, was the music, the universal idiom of the young. The genial Beatles in pudding-basin haircuts and Edwardian collars burst so freshly upon the world in 1963 that musicologists began to take pop seriously, or at least ponderously. ("'A Day in the Life' seems to proceed by offering strong simultaneous suggestions of E minor and G minor coloured by bass allusions to a foreign mode....") *The Times,* then Britain's most respected newspaper, called the Beatles the best composers of the year and marvelled how pop embraced everything – classical, oriental, folk, country music and nursery rhymes. When the Beatles released "Can't Buy Me Love," "Please Please Me," "I Want to Hold Your Hand," "Love Me Do" and the movie *A Hard Day's Night,* the *Sunday Times* lost it head and called them "the greatest composers since Beethoven."

In 1965, the year Beatlemania conquered North America and Australia and the Beatles became the first pop stars awarded MBEs by the Queen, the editor of British *Vogue* started something new by calling London "the most swinging city in the world." *Le Nouveau Candide* in Paris added that "England had given birth to a new art of living – eccentric, bohemian, simple and gay." In the United States, Roger Miller recorded his playful "England Swings" ("like a pendulum do /Bobbies on bicycles two by two"). The Rolling Stones, taking their name from Muddy Waters' Rollin' Stone Blues, toured North America billed as "the Beatles' wicked opposite numbers."

In April 1966 *Time* magazine brought all that publicity to the boil with a red-white-and-blue, ten-page cover story entitled "London, the Swinging City" written by its arts reporter Piri Halasz. "In a decade dominated by youth," she wrote, "London has burst into bloom. It swings; it is the scene.... This spring, as never before in modern times, London is switched on. Ancient elegance and new opulence are all tangled up in a dazzling blur of op and pop." Spoilsports suggested swinging London was a phony invention of promoters and copy writers, but that was only partly true. Class obsession was waning. The seeds of cultural revolution had been planted during the social levelling of World War II and the socialist government of the 1940s.

Behind the frayed facade of Victorian/Edwardian London, jazz clubs, discothèques and gambling dens were popping up like magic mushrooms. Indian and Italian restaurants proliferated. In October 2,500 people paid ten shillings to celebrate Swinging London with a marijuana-flavoured, fancy dress, all-night Pop Rave-up and Masque Drag Ball at the former railway Roundhouse on Chalk Farm Road. Sex, the contraceptive pill, the decriminalization of homosexuality, the outmoded laws on abortion and divorce were discussed in respectable newspapers and not only in the satiric *Private Eye*. Sunday afternoons were no longer grey and boring, joints no longer roasts of beef, and Carnaby Street and the King's Road were almost as famous as Piccadilly and Trafalgar Square.

The teeming boutiques were crammed with mass-produced androgynous gear: bell bottom trousers, Dutch Boy caps, PVC (polyvinyl chloride) vests and miniskirts "6 inches above the knee." Mary Quant, having popularized miniskirts, stretch stockings and "the Chelsea Look," was Queen of the Sixties and awarded the Order of the British Empire. Pete Townshend of the Who, whose trendy likeness draped in a Union Jack had appeared on the cover of *Time*, declared, "We stand for pop art clothes, pop art music, and pop art behaviour." Granny Takes a Trip, which had an automobile sticking incongruously out of its front wall, opened in the King's Road. In Kensington the art deco Biba boutique was overwhelmed with orders for yellow plastic raincoats as well as clothes that came from granny's attic.

Meantime, despite the international hype – "youth capital of Europe," "Swinging London" and so on – life continued much as usual with the important difference that some time after Margaret had left us I met the person with whom I was to spend the rest of my life, a woman with a gift of happiness. Slim, adventurous, generous and wise, Barbara Fletcher had come to London from Sault Ste. Marie in northern Ontario to teach school. We found much in common, including music, but despite all the new sounds, we and our friends spent more time in pubs like The Iron Bridge on East India Dock Road, where Queenie Watts and her eight-piece band played blues and Dixieland, than we did sampling pot or listening to "Norwegian Wood" or "Paint it Black." "Not everyone," admitted *Time,* "looks upon London's new swing as a blessing. For many who treasure an older, quieter London, the haystack hair, the suspiciously brilliant clothes, the chatter about sex and the cheery vulgarity strike an ugly contrast with the stately London that persists in the quieter squares of Belgravia or in such peaceful suburbs as Richmond. They argue that credulity and immorality, together with a sophisticated taste for the primitive, are symptoms of decadence."

Barbara and I were married in the autumn of 1965, and looking back over forty good years, the night I met Barbara Elizabeth Fletcher in the pub called The Cruel Sea in Hampstead was one of the most fortunate of my life. On the first of October Marina and Karen and a few close friends joined us at a ceremony at the Hampstead registry office. We spent our brief honeymoon in The Rose Revived by the Thames and walking the ancient green paths of the Ridgeway north of the river. When Barbara came to live with us at 14 Lyndhurst Garden, a void was filled in our lives.

So the 1960s were a tumultuous era of change, a decade of flower power, student revolt, anti-war demonstrations, the Cuban missile crisis, the CIA-inspired murder of Che Guevara, the assassination of President Kennedy, the escalation of a pointless American war in Vietnam. A hedonistic flowering of love and humanity, the '60s also spawned an increase in crime, an unexpected statistic we personally encountered in the early hours of an August morning.

Barbara and I had returned to our empty apartment late one night from a vacation in Holland, the children being away with Margaret. Sometime after midnight I was dreaming a nightmare in which a big red London bus was bearing down on me with horn blaring. Awak-

A quiet wedding at London's Hampstead registry office was attended by Marina and Karen, a dozen friends and Barbara's sister Noella, who flew from Canada with a wedding cake. Bill Bell of United Press was best man, having originally match-made the newlyweds at a pub called The Cruel Sea in Hampstead.

ing to the steady ringing of our doorbell and a searchlight beaming into our window, I opened the front door on its chain to half a dozen large grim men, some in uniform, obviously prepared to break it down. I had lived in England long enough to have lost my *Dixon of Dock Green* illusions about the kindness of British bobbies, but I was surprised they were carrying guns as they pushed their way in with the pseudo-polite way they have with the profuse use of the word Sir.

Half asleep and in pajamas I had become a dangerous suspect in a Scotland Yard manhunt. Unknown to Barbara and me, while we were in Holland hundreds of police had been searching England's railway stations, airports, docks, highways and byways for a man named Harry Roberts, a thirty-year-old career criminal "wanted for questioning" in the murder of three unarmed policemen in west London. Roberts' face had appeared in the newspapers for days with the warning "armed and dangerous," and although Roberts and I were the same height and weight and had dark hair, there the resemblance ended but he had last been seen with a small blue overnight bag just like the small blue bag sitting in my hall.

The police finally figured that the Canadian standing before them was not the London-born-and-bred Harry Roberts. They didn't apologize, but they did at least tell me why they had invaded my home. It seems a nervous neighbour had heard midnight sounds and, thinking we were still away, called the police. When the police found the real Harry Roberts, hiding in north London woods three months later and practising survival tricks learned as a soldier in the jungles of Malaya, he was sentenced to life in prison.

By 1968, the year the Beatles went to India to study transcendental meditation with the Maharishi, militant opposition to the war in Vietnam had crossed the Atlantic. On March 17, ten thousand people gathered in Trafalgar Square and marched peaceably to the American Embassy in Grosvenor Square. Both demonstrators and police were good-natured and the socialist actress Vanessa Redgrave was allowed into the embassy to deliver a formal protest, but when hotheads vandalized embassy property police on horses began pushing them back. Suddenly people began hurling stones, smoke bombs, firecrackers and scattering ball bearings under the hooves of the plunging horses. There were many injuries, but that one-day "battle of Grosvenor Square," the biggest demonstration in modern London, paled beside the 1968 student demonstrations in Paris, which grew that spring into a nationwide insurrection that nearly brought down the Charles de Gaulle government.

It had begun during the winter with conflict over scholastic issues and festered when left-wing students at the suburban University of Nanterre, led by a red-haired, twenty-three-year-old sociology student named Daniel "Danny the Red" Cohn-Bendit, added the Vietnam war to their grievances and held left-wing demonstrations on campus. When the authorities shut down classes and threatened expulsion the protests spread to the Sorbonne in central Paris. Instead of solving the problem, university administrators called in riot police with predictable results and before day's end 500 students had been arrested. When the Sorbonne suspended classes, the streets around the Latin Quarter became a nightly running battle with smoke and tear gas, the streets blocked with burned-out cars. The battle lines had been drawn with the Compagnies républicaines de sécurité (CRS), the detested anti-riot specialists bused in from rural barracks, fighting with boys and girls who were prying up paving stones and collecting junk from construction sites to build barricades.

I arrived in Paris on May 6, a beautiful spring afternoon which brought out ten thousand demonstrators organized by the unions of students and teachers protesting closure of classes and the violence of the CRS. When phalanxes of dark-blue-clad riot police fired tear-gas grenades, raised their shields, lowered their visors and charged into the crowd with truncheons, the students covered their faces with scarves and bandanas soaked in water and baking soda and counterattacked with sticks and stones. Fighting that night lasted until dawn and resulted in 422 arrests and 600 students and 345 police injured. The following day 30,000 people gathered at the Tomb of the Unknown Soldier in the Étoile to sing the "Marseillaise."

We reporters usually worked out among the demonstrators where there was drama but also a potential of getting arrested, clubbed or gassed. Few escaped burning eyes, runny noses, coughing fits, temporary blindness and disorientation. On Friday, May 10, when the fighting continued until dawn, thousands of demonstrators, bearing flags and singing, marched from Place de la République across the

France seemed on the brink of revolution as Paris students, joined by workers, battled tear gas and the notoriously tough riot police who were accused of Nazi SS brutality.

Seine bridges to occupy the streets around Boulevard St. Michel. By nightfall an estimated 20,000 citizens had gathered under the direction of parade marshals to hear speeches. Learning that the CRS, who had kept a low profile that day, were bringing in reinforcements, they feared the police were trying to seal the Latin Quarter off from the rest of the city. People began rebuilding barricades, encouraged by Fédération des étudiants revolutionnaires waving red flags.

Around midnight the rector of the Sorbonne tried to negotiate reopening of the university but when the talk ended in deadlock Danny the Red emerged to tell us there could be no peace until the police withdrew. Fighting renewed at 2 a.m. when two blue CRS buses were attacked with paving stones. The government thereupon invoked the riot act and 500 helmeted CRS advanced down Boulevard St. Michel, firing tear gas grenades and pushing everyone back and destroying barricades. The violent tide of demonstrators, shouting "fascists" and "CRS-SS," fought with sticks and stones and sang the "Internationale" and the "Marseillaise." As pandemonium spread, barricades were set on fire with gasoline and Molotov cocktails were tossed from nearby roofs. Slowly the demonstrators were forced to retreat, street after street, until they ran out of space. At dawn, Cohn-Bendit appealed to the crowds to disperse. There had been 461 arrests, including 60 "foreigners," some of whom were reporters; 367 people were injured, 60 cars burned, 128 badly damaged and streets of the Latin Quarter were a smoking desolation.

By May 13 the students who had touched off the greatest civic upheaval since the 1871 Paris Commune had won the support of the nation's workers. Two thirds of the national work force of France, including railway and airport employees, struck for better wages and working conditions and in sympathy with the students. No newspapers were published, no garbage collected. France was so paralyzed that Barbara, who had flown to join me was stranded and unable to return to our children in London. When the government announced the release of imprisoned students and the reopening of the Sorbonne the students responded by occupying university buildings and declaring the Sorbonne an autonomous "people's university." Rioting erupted again on the night of May 24, 795 people were arrested and 456 injured and attempts made to burn down the Bourse.

In June the government organized counter-demonstrations, threatened to bring in the army, reshuffled the cabinet and called an election, which President de Gaulle won by a surprisingly wide margin. The reforms that followed had a lasting impact on the rights of workers, their bargaining power, wages and pensions, as well as on the education system and scholastic freedom.

The most notable demonstration in London that autumn was an event without violence. At 10 Downing Street the writer Tariq Ali of the Vietnam Solidarity Campaign handed in a petition urging the socialist government to cease supporting the U.S. war machine. Then 25,000 marchers paraded past the American Embassy to Hyde Park to be democratically harangued at Speakers' Corner.

In January 1970 Londoners were intrigued by a new sort of pop star in the person of Pierre Elliott Trudeau, in town for a Commonwealth Conference. News filtering into the British press told of a Canada shaken out of political apathy by Trudeaumania, by Trudeau's call for a "Just Society," by Expo 67, by a renaissance in the arts, and by intense opposition to the Vietnam war which had brought Canada many bright young American immigrants.

After so many years abroad – twenty for me, nine for Barbara – Canada looked enticing though we had no intention of moving. Marina and Karen were in an excellent girl's school, Barbara was teaching at a school for boys, and London had become the one place in the world I felt homesick for when I was travelling. We were planning to buy an old house in Swain's Lane, which runs through Highgate Cemetery, where Charles Dickens's parents and Karl Marx lie buried amid stone angels and mausoleums, when I

Contact with Soviet journalists was notoriously diffficult during the Cold War but in the bar of the *Aleksandr Pushkin* we made friends with two Muscovites en route to report on America and Canada and spent amiable hours comparing notes.

was offered the job of managing director of United Press Canada based in Montreal.

Early in July 1970 Barbara, Marina, Karen and Jacky our London black cat and I sailed from London's Tilbury Docks on the *Aleksandr Pushkin,* which plied between Leningrad and Montreal via London and Cherbourg. Decorated with neo-brutalist Soviet art, served by muscular stewardesses dressed like warders, most of the tiny cabins lacked bathrooms, though she was the largest, fastest and most prestigious of the Soviet fleet. She accommodated 700 passengers and had not one class, as Marxist ideology prescribed, but two. I don't know how it happened because our passage was booked by our London office, but we had two cabins in luxury class. Jacky had a good time because the stewardesses ignored us and babied him with fresh liver on silver platters. Karen and Marina had a good time because they met other teenagers and raced around the ship at all hours doing whatever teenagers on ocean liners do. Barbara and I had a good time because we met two sociable Russian journalists, who worked for the news agency Tass and the newspaper *Izvestia* and were intrigued by Barbara's miniskirts and the fact I had once worked for Radio Free Europe. The highest point of my voyage was a surprise forty-fifth birthday party organized by Barbara, during which lights were switched off and a cake in the shape of a ship crowned with sparklers and of the colour and consistency of pumpernickel was wheeled in by waiters singing "Happy Birthday" in Russian.

On another night we dined at the captain's table on caviar, chicken Kiev, baked Alaska and iced vodka. When I cut into my chicken its buttery contents spurted onto the captain's gold braid, which is perhaps why we were invited only once. When two years later Mordecai Richler sailed to Montreal on the same ship after his twenty years in London, he complained that his first dinner on the *Aleksandr Pushkin* was overcooked spaghetti and boiled beef and wrote with an envious pen of the captain's guests consuming iced vodka, smoked surgeon, beefsteak, salad, cheese and strawberries. The *Pushkin* and her like have long since disappeared from the Atlantic, so now we must fly unless we book on a floating hotel and go for a cruise, which is not the same thing at all.

Built for the Soviet Union in East Germany in 1965, the *Aleksandr Pushkin* was one of the last liners to make regular runs across the North Atlantic. She accommodated up to 700 passengers in two classes.

13

AN UNFINISHED COUNTRY

"There is something in this native land business.... That is what makes people, makes their kind of looks, their kind of thinking, their subtlety and their stupidity, and their eating and drinking and their language." Gertrude Stein

From the deck of the *Aleksandr Pushkin* our first intimation of Canada was the aroma of spruce and pine wafting surprisingly far out to sea on the night breeze. Next morning we were in the Gulf of St. Lawrence, attended by an inquisitive school of porpoises and a sky of a clear cerulean brilliance unknown in Britain.

As we slid past Anticosti, the enigmatic island which protrudes from the St. Lawrence River like a great tongue, the rugged north shore looked much as it had, I imagined, when Jacques Cartier and Samuel Champlain sailed by; although the St. Lawrence lacked the prose and poetry of urban streams like the Thames and the Seine, it certainly had more grandeur. Up at the St. Lawrence narrows, known to Algonquians as *"hebec,"* the grey-green provincial capital was as enticing as on the November afternoon Margaret and I had sailed to England in November 1950.

My main impression on returning to Canada after more than twenty years was how much traditional British immigration was declining; the Canada I had known was rapidly becoming a nation of immigrants in a great variety of cultures, colours and creeds. Statistics Canada has since predicted that one in every three Canadians will be non-white by the year 2031.

Montreal then, with its jagged skyline, was less an American-style melting pot in 1970 than a city of ethnic layers and compartments, nourished since 1950 by the arrival of many Italian, Portuguese and Greek immigrants. Fashionable new restaurants, pharmacies, banks and boutiques had replaced ethnic mom and pop shops on the Main but happily not the Bagel Factory on nearby St. Viateur. Having lived many years in England, we were environmentally unsuited for Montreal's mid-July heat and arctic air conditioning, but Barbara and I defied the artificial chill in Dunn's Famous Smoked Meat on St. Catherine Street to introduce Karen and Marina to treats unknown in 1960s London – real hamburgers, mountainous sundaes, strawberry cheesecake, chocolate fantasies. Otherwise, we hung out in the miles of underground malls and food courts, new since my time, where the air was tolerable if unnatural.

Barbara found work at the Youth Theatre and instructing Montreal teachers in the methods and uses of drama in education, which she had learned in England. Karen was enrolled in a suburban high school where as a fourteen-year-old teenager from 1960s London she was not happy. Marina, two years older, was more comfortable in a sophisticated Quebec Cégep, one of the new junior colleges with pre-university programs. As for me, it was good to be in Montreal again although I was exasperated by the aggressive nationalism of francophone friends. They were, at the same time, the most cultivated, artistic and gracious of people and I was grateful for their French-Canadian sense of social justice and *joie de vivre* which has helped ensure that Canada is not a lesser United States. For $26,000 we bought a three-bedroom red brick house, the first home I'd ever owned, in Montreal West, an anglophone suburb right out of a 1950s *Saturday Evening Post*.

After so many years of reporting on crises abroad I had been looking forward to a placid reentry into Canadian journalism but was disconcerted by the many "For Sale" signs and graffiti – *"Québec Libre!," "Anglos Go Home!"* – which suggested 20 per cent of the city's population, my own anglophone component, might be in for troubled times.

Canadian news is as scarce in England as maple syrup, but I'd read of how the Quiet Revolution of the 1960s with its slogan *Maîtres chez nous* had freed Catholic Quebec from the heavy hand of the Church and the corrupt authoritarian rule of Premier Maurice Duplessis. In Ottawa, Prime Minister Pierre Elliott Trudeau had promised enlightened federal politics and the entrenchment of both English and French as official languages. When the Quebec Liberal Party won an election the Toronto *Globe and Mail* declared, "The province of Quebec is alive and well in Canada." I'd seen brief items in the British press of sporadic terrorist bombings during the 1960s, but distance had diminished their impact. Since my return in July, there had been no incidents, so I was unprepared for the headlines of the next eighty-four days, a defining time in Canadian history.

I arrived at work on the cool autumnal Monday morning of October 5 to the news of a threatened doctors' strike over the introduction of Medicare. Canada seemed peaceable. Around ten o'clock the phones started ringing and we set to work preparing a sketchy report on the abduction of someone I'd never heard of before: forty-nine-year-old James R. "Jasper" Cross, the British resident trade commissioner, from his Westmount home on Redpath Crescent. According to his terrified maid, while Montreal was eating breakfast two armed, masked men rang the doorbell, pushed into the house, handcuffed Cross, wrapped him in a blanket and bundled the mild-manner victim into a taxi cab after allowing his wife to kiss him goodbye. One of them said, "We are the FLQ."

The use of a common LaSalle Company taxi in broad daylight seemed unreal, even comic. But by mid-afternoon the first numbered "communiqués" sent to French-language radio station CKAC firmly identified the kidnappers – including the rogue taxi driver – as the Liberation cell of the Front de libération du Québec (FLQ), the shadowy young Marxists who had been demanding Quebec's separation. Che Guevara was their idol and their inflammatory bible *Nègres blancs d'amérique,* in which Montreal journalist Pierre Vallières equated francophones with the Blacks of the American south. Vallières had written "the workers of Quebec are aware of their condition as niggers, exploited men, second-class citizens. Have they not been, ever since the establishment of the New France in the seventeenth century, the servants of the imperialists, the white niggers?"

At 3 p.m. Quebec justice minister Jérôme Choquette called a press conference to divulge the ransom demands: $500,000 in gold, release of twenty-three "political prisoners" (who had been found guilty of criminal acts), the publication of an FLQ manifesto, cessation of police searches and a plane to fly the kidnappers to Cuba. The authorities tried to stop its publication, fearing support of FLQ aims might lead to insurrection. Certainly when it was broadcast by CKAC, which became an FLQ mail drop, the long manifesto with its charges of social injustice tapped a deep well of francophone resentment. "The Front de libération du Québec is a group of Québec workers who have decided to use every means to make sure that the people of Québec take control of their destiny," it began. "The FLQ wants the total independence of all Québécois, united in a free society, purged forever of the clique of voracious sharks, the big bosses and their henchmen who have made Québec their hunting preserve for cheap labour and unscrupulous exploitation."

The following week was one of rumour, anxiety and frustration. None of the thirty suspects recently arrested had anything to do with the kidnapping and news stories were based on FLQ communiqués. At 5:30 p.m. Saturday, October 10, the drama seemed to be reaching a denouement because Choquette, who had summoned me to Quebec City to lecture UPI for disseminating FLQ communications, had convoked another press conference. If the FLQ released

Cross unharmed the kidnappers would be granted free passage to Cuba but not the twenty-three "political prisoners," a sticking point throughout the crisis. "No society can consent," he said, "to have the decisions of its judicial and government institutions challenged or set aside by the blackmail of a minority, for that signifies the end of all social order."

Choquette had hardly finished speaking when the FLQ struck at the heart of the provincial government by kidnapping the deputy premier and labour minister, forty-nine-year-old Pierre Laporte. Laporte had been playing catch with his nephew beside his suburban St-Hubert home when he was bundled into a car by two armed masked men. Suddenly it seemed the FLQ could kidnap at will. In Montreal West that Saturday night Barbara worried they now might kidnap journalists.

Next morning Laporte's kidnappers revealed they were the FLQ Chenier cell, named for a martyr of Quebec's 1837 rebellion, and warned Laporte would die if their demands were not met. Premier Robert Bourassa revealed the contents of a piteous "Dear Robert" letter in which Laporte wrote, "I am treated well, even courteously. The power to decide over my life is in your hands. If ... the sacrifice of my life would bring good results, one could accept it ... but I remain alone as the head of a large family."

On October 15, in an event reminiscent of the May 1968 student uprising Paris, three thousand students staged a rally in Montreal's Paul Sauvé arena to support the FLQ manifesto, fuelling the government's fear, which only later seemed like paranoia, of a widespread insurrection. Choquette was rumoured to be packing a pearl-handled revolver. Premier Bourassa was isolated on the top floor of the Queen Elizabeth Hotel, where his cabinet was meeting day and night. Montreal's emotional mayor, Jean Drapeau, declared: "The revolution in Quebec is in full execution. The situation is dangerous. The population has no idea of the gravity of the moment ... [which] eerily resembles revolutions in other countries." Jean Marchand, senior Quebec-based federal cabinet minister and former labour leader, reckoned FLQ membership at a thousand with "thousands of guns, rifles, machine guns and bombs and about 2000 pounds of dynamite."

With the police clearly unable to cope, Bourassa called on the federal government to send in a thousand battle-ready soldiers of the francophone Royal 22nd Regiment to protect public buildings and politicians and also issued an ultimatum. If the FLQ agreed, his government would assure the kidnappers safe passage to Cuba and recommend release of five of the twenty-three "political prisoners." When no reply was forthcoming, Trudeau in Ottawa abandoned his well-known role of civil libertarian and declared martial law by invoking, on the first occasion in peacetime, the War Measures Act, in which civil liberties were suspended and FLQ supporters arrested simply on suspicion of taking part in "an apprehended insurrection." Nearly 500 people, most of them francophone, none of them kidnappers, were detained without warrant: journalists, broadcasters, writers, actors, singers, community organizers, doctors, educators, students and members of the legal (if separatist) Parti Québécois. All but a few were released without charge.

Anglophones across the country massively supported Trudeau's decision. Terrorism effectively ceased, and as slowly became apparent, the FLQ turned out to be a small, amateurish, squabbling, loosely organized group. Only nine had taken part in the kidnappings. As Jacques Lanctôt, one of the Cross kidnappers, said later, "We were romantics. We saw ourselves going off to war, though we didn't really know what we were doing. We wanted to make a revolution, but we didn't want to kill anyone." Their major weapon was the miasmic fear they were able to create with help from student rallies and citizens, no one seemed to know how many.

But on Sunday, October 18, the mood in francophone Quebec

changed to shock, revulsion and sorrow. The FLQ had gone too far. Early that morning the body of Pierre Laporte was found in the trunk of an abandoned car not far from his home. According to the coroner, Laporte had been strangled by his own medallion chain, but whether his death was deliberate or the accidental outcome of a struggle to escape, as some suggested, hardly mattered. Francophones had had enough; political violence was supplanted by the democratic processes of the separatist Parti Québécois with its ties to militant labour unions and social democratic ideology. Led by the charismatic former broadcaster René Lévesque, the PQ opposed Trudeau's vision of a multicultural, unified, bilingual Canada, but elsewhere Trudeau emerged from the October Crisis with 90 per cent poll approval across the country. The following year his marriage to twenty-two-year-old Margaret Sinclair revived waning Trudeaumania.

In December 1970, two months after the abduction of James Cross, police found the flat where he was held and rescued him. As promised, his kidnappers were granted a plane flight to Cuba, where they lived for a while before going to Paris, eventually returning to Canada, where they served terms of imprisonment. Paul Rose, his brother Jacques Rose and Francis Simard, the abductors of Pierre Laporte, were found hiding in a tunnel on a farm and served long prison terms before being paroled in the 1980s.

The cathartic emotions unleashed by the crisis confounded extreme separatists by having the long-term effect of holding Quebec inside confederation. In a province of six million where five million were francophone, the struggle now became one about which language would dominate, as Quebec introduced language laws such as Bill 101 that made English public signs illegal – even the use of the anglophone apostrophe and the STOP on the STOP/ARRET street signs. With such laws and the departure of many head offices and some 150,000 disaffected Montreal anglophones to Ontario and elsewhere, French regained the dominance it had lost two centuries earlier. The aim, we were told, was to make Montreal as "French" as Toronto was "English," though paradoxically Montreal was to become more rather than less multicultural due to the constant influx of immigrants.

The October crisis had reawakened anxieties about national identity and our relationship with the United States, which remained benignly ignorant of its northern neighbour while controlling many of our industries. It was not just that America had influence but that Canada, as *Harper's Magazine* observed at the time, was "encrusted" with American initiative and thought, economically and culturally. When I was a child, American radio and "the funny papers" – newspaper comics – influenced my world for better or worse; these days the impact of American television has clearly become much greater. In Ottawa, a Senate Committee on Mass Media deplored the influence of imported news produced by and for Americans with no reference to Canadian culture or history. Having worked for American news organizations for twenty-five years, I had personally come to believe the survival of United Press International in Canada depended on making it more obviously Canadian. At that time most of the news, sports and news photos we were dispensing to our Canadian clients originated in the United States.

Since 1950 UPI Canada had shrunk. Although the sole competitor of the Canadian Press agency, instead of its former one hundred UPI employees with bureaus in all major cities and clients from Halifax to Vancouver, there now were twenty-five employees with a clientele concentrated in Montreal, Ottawa and Toronto. This was largely due to media consolidation and the resulting elimination of competition.

When the ninety-year-old *Toronto Telegram,* whose editor Arnold Agnew was a friend from UP London days, shut down in November 1970 I was relieved to hear its staff were launching a new daily newspaper. Since they would need a wire service and CP was unavailable to them for contractual reasons, they would be obliged to turn to United Press International. I was less enthusiastic when I heard that the new daily was to be a tabloid in the tradition of Rupert Murdoch, the Australian who had been dubbed "the Dirty Digger" when he'd recently launched the cheesecake-and-sensation *Sun* newspaper in London. UPI Canada was already serving a French-language paper of that nature in Montreal – Pierre Péladeau's *Journal de Montréal* – and I'd hoped the genre would not take root in English Canada.

However, the *Sun* shone not only in Toronto but spread the franchise successfully to Calgary, Edmonton and Ottawa. Since UPI needed the money to survive, I sold the *Toronto Sun* our service. Ironically, some time after I'd left UPI it was to be the thriving *Toronto Sun,* rather than an older established newspaper, which became the organization that realized my hope of turning UPI Canada into a fully Canadian agency. With *Sun* backing, the new all-Canadian UPI Canada lasted until 1985 when it was sold to CP. By that time the New York-based United Press International, our parent company, had gone bankrupt and was sold for one dollar to two entrepreneurs who had no experience in running a news organization. During the next two decades UPI was sliced up, drawn and quartered, and resold so many times it became unrecognizable. The bones having been picked, what was left was bought, not by Conrad Black, who reportedly made a bid for it, but News World Communications, which to the dismay of UPI employees was an arm of Sun Myong Moon's Unification Church, "the Moonies," known for their mass weddings. UPI these days calls itself a "global information service" and bears no relation, except in name, to the organization I left thirty years ago. The Toronto-based Sun newspaper group has been sold to Péladeau's Quebecor empire in Montreal.

By 1975, having had thirty years of news work at home and abroad, I wanted to try something else, and travelling through Canada I had

O.M.

3744 PARC LAFONTAINE.
AUGUST 1984.

Our third-floor flat on avenue du Parc Lafontaine sported one of Montreal's steep and distinctive outdoor iron staircases, quaint but hazardous in icy weather.

learned how much oral history remained unpublished. I was fifty years old. If I were to start a new career it should be now. Barbara had become a professor in the drama department of Concordia University, Karen was completing university in England and Marina was back in London, having finished university in Quebec. The time was propitious and the nudge came from my father-in-law, Gordon Fletcher, as we sat on the veranda of the family camp one afternoon at Wigwam Bay on the northeastern shores of Lake Superior.

In 1921 Gordon had come from Liverpool, England, at the age of nine to live with his English mother and Canadian stepfather in the Pukaskwa lumber camps, 150 miles up Lake Superior north of Sault Ste. Marie. In his teens he became camp clerk in a wilderness of hills, rivers and spruce trees so remote the only links with the outside world from December to April were Eric Skead's dog team, which mushed seventy trackless miles to the railway town of White River every fortnight.

In 1976, before Pukaskwa was opened as a national park, Gordon and I went in on a Parks Canada launch and found the moldering logs of the cabin at Imogene Creek that had been his boyhood home, immortalized by an A.Y. Jackson painting called Bear Cabin. Gordon said, "I guess someone coming along now would see the remains of our camps and wonder what sort of men worked there and who we were." Though local histories across the country have sometimes included accounts of woodsmen, I was surprised no one had written a national book about one of Canada's most famous trades. Inspired by Gordon's stories of logging along the northern shores of Lake Superior I quit UPI, sold our suburban home, moved into a downtown Montreal flat and, with the support of Barbara, Marina and Karen, began a new career which produced *The Lumberjacks* and nine other books of non-fiction social history.

14

TELLING TALES

The Lumberjacks was published by McGraw-Hill Ryerson in the autumn of 1976, a fortunate time for aspiring authors because several new Canadian publishers had recently appeared and McGraw-Hill of New York had purchased the ailing 140-year-old Ryerson Press of Toronto and was expanding its list.

There were far fewer authors than now, as I recall, and more unexplored subjects. The Canada Council for the Arts had begun encouraging new writers through its Explorations program, and though an author's standard royalty of 10 per cent is no way to get rich, the Council had made it easier to earn a living. Apart from natural egoism and the need to earn money common to all trades and professions, the dominant motive for writing books tends to differ from writer to writer. For some there is the joy of words, for some the impulse to share experience and impressions, for others an effort to alter political beliefs. The old also write for posterity.

Despite my reduced income it was exhilarating to be my own boss, free from round-the-clock demands of breaking news. For thirty years I'd been accustomed to writing something every working day of my life whether I felt like it or not, which was good training for the marathon of writing a book. The only book I had authored until then was an historical novel, *Lord of the Sea,* based on the 16th-century adventures of the irascible Vasco da Gama and his gentle brother Paulo in discovering the sea route to the spice-rich Indies, thereby creating the basis of a powerful Portuguese empire. Written in the 1950s in Lisbon after I had learned enough Portuguese to read archival records, my never-quite-finished tale of international intrigue and brutally unequal sea and land battles between well-armed crusading Christians and poorly-armed Moslems gathers dust unpublished on my shelf. In the dark ages before computers, I had to type multiple revisions of my various manuscripts on a clunky manual Underwood; thus when desk-top computers arrived, writing a book became more like cabinet-making and less like coal mining. The process of smoothing a knotty rough patch here, honing a sharp edge there – creating an artifact – became as pleasurable as research, archival detective work, and the subsidized travel to interview interesting people.

As noted in the previous chapter, I'd been inspired to write *The Lumberjacks* by Barbara's father, Gordon Fletcher, a logging camp veteran, but in fact I found I'd married into a whole family prepared to encourage my project and provide me with logging contacts. Barbara's grandparents and two generations of uncles and cousins had lived and worked in the northern Ontario bush and Barbara herself had spent her earliest years in the 1930s and early 40s with her mother Ethel

and sister Karen in isolated pulpwood camps like Magpie and Minnapuka amid miles of spruce, fir and jack pine, reached only by water or by railway (CPR, CNR, Algoma Central) stretching north over the hills from Wawa, Hawk Junction, White River and

With father-in-law Gordon Fletcher at the door of the cabin where Gordon lived as a boy newly arrived from England, when the wilderness Pukaskwa logging depot served 300 men.

Gordon and Ethel Fletcher and children Barbara (above right) and Karen lived six years in remote Ontario logging camps north of Sault Ste. Marie, Ontario. Families were rarities in lumber camps.

Oba. Barbara's introduction to education at the age of five consisted of an Ontario government correspondence course and an illustrated four-cent primer, *Mary, John and Peter,* which contained, along with a narrative, a series of questions. ("Is Jack Frost black? Is a Christmas tree red?") Her answers ("No" in both cases) were dispatched on one of the trains which daily came through and were marked by someone in Toronto and returned with gold or red stars depending on how successfully she had formed her letters.

There were few women in Canadian camps but I met wives of logging contractors who had lived in remote Pukaskwa. Mrs. Tim Devon told me, "I was happy in there and I used to think 'This is what I call pioneering.' Being the only woman and having small children you kept pretty much to yourself and kept the children away.

You take men cooped up from September to May, there were little problems here and there." Ida Lefebvre, when a sedate white-haired grandmother living in the Soo, told me, "There were times I skidded logs for my husband Joe…. I would get six or seven logs chained together and skid them 500 feet to the river. Sometimes I'd jump on a log and ride it. When you are young, the things you do!"

By train, bus, car, truck, boat, plane and helicopter, for the two years I worked on *The Lumberjacks* I toted a tape recorder from the Atlantic to the Pacific and north to the tree line where the tundra begins. In cottages, retirement homes, motels, beer parlours and boarding houses I interviewed 130 veteran loggers and their wives, many of whom were in their eighties or older. Their memories of being youngsters were much sharper than those of their middle years, they told me, because young experience was less cluttered. Seen in sepia photographs, their old lumber camps suggested the romance of sailing ships and times more simple and vivid. Whether Nova Scotia shantymen, Ontario lumberjacks, Quebec *bucherons* or British Columbia loggers, most had been farm boys in an age when logging was their only winter work. Like sailors and cowboys they created traditions and legends and told their stories with wit and humour. Their year began in the fall when the farmer's year was ending. Once suitable wood was located, men with five-pound poll axes, two-man crosscut saws and bucksaws went in.

It was, they told me, a poor camp that lacked its own Bull of the Woods. "Old-time foremen were self-made men, worked up from the axe, never asked a man to do something they couldn't do themselves," said Geoff Randolph, who hailed from New Brunswick. The foreman was like a captain of a ship and his word was law. Larry Frost on the Ottawa River could "run faster, jump higher and spit farther than any son of a bitch in camp." Fightin' Fint Brophy, who worked for Jabez Snowball on the Miramichi River, and red-wigged, 220-pound Hank Phelan in British Columbia kept order with their fists. In Ontario, George "Cockeye" McNee of Arnprior got his nickname by calling everything he didn't like "cockeyed" but no one knew how "Cruel Face" McKinnon got his nickname, for "though he wasn't good lookin' he was a pleasant fella." Bob Smith at Blind River was called "Moonlight Smith" because he kept his men working late. Arriving in camp, the first thing lumberjacks asked was, "Who's the foreman?" The second was, "Who's the cook?"

In the primitive white pine lumber camps early in the 20th century bunks were "two-man muzzle loaders where you woke up with your hair froze to the rough log wall," said Geoff Randolph. Sickness? "Gentle, gentle! You laid there and doctored yourself with Buckley's Mixture, or the cook might mix up some concoction of ginger. They had Dr. Daniel's Colic Cure for the horses, good for man or beast." Dinner might be salt pork and beans followed by molasses pie, cooked in iron pots over an open hearth.

After the camps improved and imported stoves, the meals improved. Dinner might be pea soup, roast beef or pork, potatoes, peas, rice pudding, fresh-baked bread, butter, cheese, pies, cookies; breakfast could be oatmeal porridge, stewed prunes, pork and beans, maybe steak, toast, raisin pie, ginger cake, bread and butter, tea or coffee. No alcohol was tolerated for obvious reasons, and the custom was to eat silently and quickly. "We had more trouble with cooks than with anyone else," allowed foreman Vic Hamilton of Chapleau. "It was a seven-day-a-week job, early and late." The first to start work at 4 a.m. by the light of kerosene lamps, the cook was the last into bed. In the cold months after Christmas, teamsters arrived with their oxen or farm horses to skid the logs along roads built of snow and ice. "Some of those old skidding horses were as wise as the men who drove them," recalled Jim MacDonald of Thessalon in northern Ontario. There were few places a horse could not go, and in those places they were fitted with wooden snowshoes. Spring was the season of the river drivers with spiked boots, peaveys, pike poles and dynamite, who broke log jams and sluiced wood for miles to the mills. A white-water man could run and dance along a log and leap to another when it started to sink, and on the Miramichi their boots were hung on trees to mark where they drowned. Nowadays logs are hauled by truck and the last big drive was on Quebec's Coulonge River in 1982.

On the British Columbia rain coast, where the warmer climate permitted logging all year, Douglas fir and red cedar grew so high and thick that loggers from "down east" had to learn new skills and steam logging transformed the woods into outdoor factories with donkey engines and narrow-gauge railways. A 250-ton Lidgerwood Skidder powered a "sky line," which was hung like a clothesline between two tall spar trees by a high-rigger. "Sometimes a spar tree would break," a high-rigger told me, "and everything would come crashing down all around you." The B.C. poet Peter Trower, a logger himself, called it a battlefield: "... blood can spill upon the forest floor, and logging can be very like a war."

When *The Lumberjacks* was published I was introduced to the usual author's tour of national media and bookstore signings. Interviews were mostly early breakfast-time shows but enjoyable so long as the coffee was fresh and the interviewer had taken the trouble to read the book. Signings on the other hand could be deflating. A signing for my book *Scotland Farewell: The People of the Hector* had been announced with a nice half-page ad in a Halifax daily paper, the event to be at Simpson's department store, where I had long ago worked as a holiday stockboy. When I arrived at the big store on the afternoon of October 31 they seated me behind a faux antique desk between a Halloween candy display and the furniture department, presumably because there was no proper book section. There was brisk trade at the orange- and black-draped candy counter behind me but only half a dozen timid book lovers straggled in and I had to disappoint one rural-looking gent who had seen the advertisement and wondered if I was by any chance his long-lost cousin. After a quiet two hours I was about to call it a day when approached by an old lady who had been eyeing me purposefully from behind a dresser. I flashed my best smile, anticipating a sale. She was not amused. "Young man," she said, "how much is the desk?" When I admitted I didn't know, she sniffed impatiently and hurried off to find someone who did, or maybe to complain about my incompetence.

This being my first published book, I awaited reviews with some natural apprehension but happily they were favourable. The Book of the Month Club made it one of their selections, the Canadian Book Review Annual called it "a fascinating tale of Canada in its growing up stages," the *Ottawa Citizen* had "high praise [for] the first national history of the lumberjacks." Commenting on the oral history content *Atlantic Insight* said: "It is marvellous material of the type often ignored by historians." *Canadian Geographic Journal* said the book "put readers right beside the lumberjacks, allowing them to feel the bite of the axe, taste the baked beans, live the terror of the log jam."

To my surprise it was one of two runners-up for the $25,000 Governor General's Award for Non-fiction in 1978. One of the three judges, a B.C. history professor, wrote that it was "a superb marriage of text and pictures ... nostalgic but not sentimental," but the award went to *Go-Boy! Memories of a Life Behind Bars,* a sensational account by recidivist Roger Caron of his thirty-five years in prison, with a foreword by Pierre Berton.

The Lumberjacks evidently touched susceptibilities, for soon after it appeared I received the first of several invitations to write more forest history, starting with Anticosti, the mysterious island I'd glimpsed while sailing home through the Gulf of St. Lawrence on the *Aleksandr Pushkin* in 1970. The biggest privately owned island in the world, Anticosti had been logged for fifty years by a Montreal pulp and paper company, which was then in the process of selling it to the province of Quebec. Bigger than Prince Edward Island, Anticosti, which was the white man's name for the Montagnais *Natiscouisti,* "hunting ground of the bear," was a 19th-century graveyard where hundreds of ships bound to or from Montreal were wrecked on limestone reefs. A Canadian anomaly, independent of federal and provincial governments, it had experienced two failed efforts by private companies to colonize the island with fishing and farming before it was purchased in 1895 by "the Chocolate King of France."

Many dream of owning an island, but Henri Menier, a rich candymaker with an engineering degree, made his dream a reality by becoming the autocratic Grand Seigneur of a personal fief. The bearded Parisian bachelor spent a small fortune building roads, railways, an experimental farm, the model village of Port Menier and a fanciful four-storey, thirty-room wooden chateau with baronial hall and stained glass windows. In his 800-ton yacht he brought European friends to fish for salmon in the Jupiter River and hunt in his seaside kingdom consisting of woods, rivers and a waterfall higher than Niagara. He began tinkering with the ecosystem by importing mainland moose, elk, buffalo, reindeer, foxes and 220 white-tailed deer, while forbidding the island's 300 residents, most of them his employees, the right to hunt, fish, own guns and dogs or drink alcohol.

To get some return on this expensive hobby, Menier hired Finnish lumberjacks to harvest spruce and fir and was planning a pulp mill when he died at the untimely age of sixty. While it is intriguing to imagine the private state-within-a-state Anticosti might have become had Menier lived, his disapproving brother came from Paris and sold the island in 1927 to a pulp and paper company that turned Port Menier into a glorified lumber camp while developing a lucrative sideline in wealthy Americans who paid large fees to fish for teeming salmon and shoot the tame white-tailed deer, which had multiplied like rabbits. In 1974 the island Menier had bought for $125,000 was sold to the Quebec government for $26 million and converted into a provincial park. These days Anticosti is advertised on the internet as "this mysteriously enchanting island … where impressive cliffs plunge into the sea and canyons, waterfalls, lakes, and majestic rivers rival for attention with the abundant and varied fauna." Henri Menier's Parisian friends might feel at home, except that they would not be so luxuriously accommodated. The magnificent chateau, used to store hay and having fallen into disrepair and become a fire hazard, was deliberately burned down one October afternoon in 1953.

Although I'd had no intention of specializing in forestry, a Vancouver history buff who read *The Lumberjacks* wrote to me suggesting a book about the company he had recently joined as a senior executive. Since it was MacMillan Bloedel, the biggest forest company in British Columbia, and research and writing would take all of two years, I would have to live part of that time in Vancouver. Though Barbara was now a professor in the Concordia University Department of Theatre in Montreal and could not join me often, we agreed the book was an opportunity that should not be missed.

Having obtained an assurance of editorial freedom and access to company records and a contract to "research and write a factually accurate and impartial history … within the framework of a general history of the industry and the province," I began work in 1980 on *Empire of Wood: The MacMillan Bloedel Story.* Barbara joined me that summer in a rented apartment in Vancouver before returning to Montreal for her fall term. Vancouver with its forests, mountains and sea being the most splendidly livable city I'd ever known, I spent every weekend I could hiking, biking, swimming at Wreck Beach and in winter cross-country skiing up in Manning Park.

British Columbia's rough-and-tumble lumber industry is synonymous with that province's history, but despite its wealth of, literally, awesome trees, logging came late because of the distance around Cape Horn from Britain, which had long been the 19th-century lumber market for eastern Canada. For decades lumber in B.C. was a poor fourth after mining, farming and fishing; only with the arrival of the Canadian Pacific Railway in 1886 did the industry improve, though its greatest growth would await the arrival of Harvey Reginald MacMillan half a century later.

Over six feet tall, 200 pounds, with a bushy brow and keen blue eyes, while no Paul Bunyan, MacMillan was one of those people who give an illusion of being larger than life. Addicted to work, he rarely drank, never smoked and was both admired and feared as a hard driver. He had come to British Columbia in 1915 as a government forester, which gave him invaluable knowledge of the woodlands, and in 1919 at the age of thirty-four established MacMillan Export Company, which introduced the province to the British and Japanese markets. He bought up timberlands and diversified his company by acquisitions and mergers and in 1931 the *Financial Times* called MacMillan "the No. 1 industrialist and business leader of British Columbia." Born of a poor Ontario farm family, MacMillan was once portrayed by his cousin, novelist Mazo de la Roche, as "tender and hard, imaginative and stolid, pugnacious and yielding, lovable and cold." He did, however, have the ability to laugh at himself. Vancouver historian Barry Broadfoot told me he was at a reception when a business reporter from the *Vancouver Sun* got up the courage after a few drinks to do a little tycoon baiting.

"Do you know what they say about you, Mr. MacMillan?" the reporter asked.

"No," said MacMillan. "What do they say about me."

"Well, they say you're a buccaneer."

MacMillan laughed with delight. "That's me, I sink 'em without a trace."

But seven years after merging his firm with Bloedel Stewart and Welch to create the nation's biggest forest products corporation, Canada's most successful lumberman surprised the business community by anointing an unlikely successor, a Supreme Court judge whose only business experience had been a youthful summer job stacking lumber. Whereas MacMillan had anchored his business in Canada, the forceful J.V. Clyne, like MacMillan a hard-headed Scot, brought in an American management consulting firm with a team of MBAs and began to diversify and expand into the United States, Europe and Australia. Eventually the company ran into difficulties and shortly before MacMillan died in his ninety-first year in 1976 it suffered losses, and the story became one of boardroom battles and takeover bids as well as acquisitions and expansions. In the final year of the 20th century the company H.R. MacMillan built was sold to Weyerhaeuser of Federal Way, Washington, which had become interested not because of "Macblo's" Canadian operations but because of the Canadian company's American assets, which had been part of the multinational expansions begun under J.V. Clyne.

Empire of Wood: The MacMillan Bloedel Story was completed with the assistance of Emily Samson Courtright, the corporation archivist, and published by Douglas and McIntyre of Vancouver in the autumn of 1982 and in the United States by the University of Washington Press. The December 1983 issue of *Canadian Book Review* said, "Commissioned corporate stories are often suspect, as they present a limited view of the corporation; but *Empire of Wood* is one of the best stories written on a Canadian corporation." Barry Broadfoot wrote to say, "I ... enjoyed it very much ... [but] I'm surprised you made no mention of Miss [Dorothy] Dee, the world's most formidable private secretary, who protected H.R. as if he were the crown jewels."

I often wished I'd met MacMillan, not only because it would have improved the book but because of our shared Scottish heritage and the coincidence that he and I had both grown up without a father and had to overcome tuberculosis when young. A complex man remembered for philanthropy and such institutions as Vancouver's

H.R. MacMillan Space Centre, MacMillan was neither a typical tycoon nor dogmatic capitalist. As a young man in the 1920s he had pioneered sustainable forestry in a world where the history of forests, whether in China, Africa or Europe, had been disastrous. "From planes, roads, railways we see the green forest and think all is well," MacMillan wrote in 1959, "[but] nowhere else in the free world has so little been done for so large and valuable a permanent forest area as in Canada."

Politicians had apparently assumed that education rather than regulation would save our forests, but twenty-five years after Mac-Millan's warning little had changed as white-haired loggers I interviewed spoke of the vast difference between the forests they knew as young men and the shrunken forests of today. It was widely acknowledged that Canadian forests had been exploited rather than managed and ill-advised methods of clear cutting, the large-scale felling of trees at the expense of the ecosystem, had been all too common. As part of a widespread effort to promote sustainable forestry, with the backing of concerned professional foresters I spent a year researching and writing *Heritage Lost: The Crisis in Canada's Forests*. "It demonstrates," said one reviewer, "how ignorance of the true condition of the nation's forests has caused the general public, and shortsighted politicians and businessmen, to remain unaware that the continuing degradation of the country's forest may make it impossible to reverse the damage being done. Instead of mining forests, industry and government must treat them like a renewable heritage through programs of sustained yield wherein balance is achieved between growth and harvest rates." Today, a quarter century after the book appeared, Canada claims to be a world leader in sustainable forest management. By law, forests harvested on public lands, which account for most of our woodlands, must be replaced but there is still ample evidence that managing our forests to maintain sustainable ecosystems will be an ongoing challenge.

*   *   *

It was inevitable that I write about railways. Like most small-town boys I'd been thrilled by the sooty black monsters that steamed and whistled through Windsor and across the countryside, fetching food and mail-order purchases. They brought news, romance, sophistication and "hotels on wheels" – dining cars with snowy table cloths and shiny silverware, and sleeping cars finished in dark mahogany, upholstered in grey, blue and brown, named for Canadian cities. My maternal great-grandfather had been a railway conductor, one of my grandfathers was a railway engineer and the other a station master, both employed by the Dominion Atlantic Railway (DAR), which became part of the Canadian Pacific Railway (CPR). My grandmother's uncle, the curiously-named Thomas Gotobed McMullen, whom I have mentioned previously, had added to his lumber empire by building a fifty-mile railway from Truro to Windsor.

There have many books about the privately owned CPR, a company adept at pubic relations, but few about less-showy pioneer railways, the Grand Trunk and Canadian Northern, which united to form the CPR's competitor, the Canadian National Railway (CNR), our first crown corporation. Aided and abetted by Ken MacKenzie, an historian and CNR corporate archivist, I began a long-term project which resulted in three books.

The People's Railway: A History of Canadian National told of its debt-ridden birth in 1919 through its struggles to make a profit while furthering the national development policies of the government of the day. The dynamic if tragic CNR president hired in 1922 by Prime Minister Mackenzie King was a big, likeable American who'd won his spurs by saving a failing railway in England, for which he was knighted. During the next decade Sir Henry W. Thornton transformed the CNR from a struggling freight line into a profitable modern railway. Spending money to make money, Thornton

With Ken MacKenzie,CN archivist. *The Asian Dream* told the story of how Canadian National Railways opened a trade route to the Orient via Prince Rupert in competiton with the CPR, whose traditional port was farther south in Vancouver.

built a passenger service with trains such as the Super Continental and Continental Limited, a chain of luxury hotels and a fleet of ocean liners. He introduced diesel locomotives to Canada and on-board radio programs with a network that was the forerunner of the Canadian Broadcasting Corporation. But by 1932 Thornton and his expansionist polices had become victims of partisan politics and the Great Depression. What had been hailed as progressive by Mac-kenzie King's Liberals was called extravagant by the Conservatives who had ousted King from government. The ailing Thornton was denounced, maliciously forced to resign and died a year later at the age of sixty-three. After his death his contribution to the nation was recognized and his reputation restored.

A second book, *The Asian Dream: The Pacific Rim and Canada's National Railway,* was written in the 1970s at a time north-south rail traffic with the United States had long dwarfed Canada's historic nation-building east-west flow. *The Asian Dream* told of how CN's ancestors, the Grand Trunk and Canadian Northern, built tracks across the northern prairies (CPR being farther south) to the Pacific coast. Asian Pacific trade having been the prize when explorers sought the elusive Northwest Passage, the railways had the Far East in mind when they built their "land bridge," in the old imperial dream of "an all red route" by ship-rail-ship from Britain to China and Japan. The northern B.C. port of Prince Rupert was meant to rival Vancouver and Seattle, and though east-west shipments of Canadian commodities did increase they never began to match those flowing south and north.

It was only in the 1970s that Prime Minister Pierre Trudeau restored life to the Asian dream when he decided that trade with the Asian Pacific might rescue Canada from excessive reliance on one market, that of the United States. As an instrument of government, CN became a leading actor in the effort to build up Pacific Rim trade. But, such being the vanity of human wishes, by the 21st century, twenty years after *The Asian Dream* was published, Canadian trade with the United States had grown bigger than ever and an equivalence in Asian trade remained a dream. In 1995 CN, having sold its commuter lines, hotels and other non-rail enterprises, returned to its roots as a freight carrier. CN having secured tracks in the United States as far south as the Gulf of Mexico, U.S. trade was accounting for half of the railway's business. But what else, as they say, is new? In commerce, as in popular culture, sports and national defence – the list is long – America has been lapping at our sovereign shores in a rising tide all my life

A third CN book, co-authored with Lorne Perry, was *Train Country*, described by *Canadian Geographic* of May 1995 as linking in photos and text "the story of the CNR to the development of Canada itself: the settlement of the Prairies; the discovery of mineral wealth in the North; the war effort in the 1940s; the effect of cars, buses and commercial airline travel on passenger rail service; and, ultimately,

One of the few Montreal Square Mile houses renovated for modern office use was the 19th-century limestone home of Dr. William A. Molson at the corner of Sherbrooke Street and McGill College Avenue. Reading *The Square Mile* inspired the head of a company to restore the house as its Canadan office.

the rationalization of railways in the 1990s in a fiercely competitive North American transportation market."

The Square Mile: Merchant Princes of Montreal, with a theme suggested by the collection of William Notman photos in the McCord Museum, was completed in 1987. By that time most of Montreal's "golden Square Mile," as some called it, had changed almost beyond recognition and lived on in old photos, although bits of hammer-dressed stone and sculpted decoration might conceivably be found amid the burgeoning excavations for the city's office blocks.

In the late 1970s I had returned to Nova Scotia to complete *Scotland Farewell: The People of the Hector,* published in 1980. Like *The Lumberjacks* it was a runner-up for the Governor General's award, won by Jeffrey Simpson's *Discipline of Power,* a book about Ottawa politics. I consoled myself with the thought that two "runners up" just might conceivably equal one winner but the $25,000 would have come in handy.

Among the pleasures of writing has been the support of old friends and the vision of new ones. Though a Nova Scotia-born Scot, I had known nothing of the harrowing voyage of the pioneers who sailed to Pictou from the Highlands on the leaky brig *Hector* in 1773; until, that is, my friend Clyde Sanger of Ottawa, British-born journalist and author, suggested I write about them. Clyde had not realized then that one of his own ancestors had been on the ship, but while touring Nova Scotia had seen in a bank lobby in Pictou an exhibition of children's drawings celebrating the 200th anniversary of the *Hector*'s arrival.

Clyde's suggestion was daunting. The *Hector*'s passenger list, assuming there had been one, had not survived, though forty years after the brig's arrival two aging survivors had compiled lists from memory which did not always agree. Most of the nearly 200 immigrants were obscure Gaelic-speaking crofters or artisans who left no written records, but at the Nova Scotia Archives in Halifax I found encouragement. In 1870 the Rev. Dr. George Patterson, grandson of a *Hector* passenger, had included *Hector* people in his *History of the County of Pictou*. While regretting the difficulties in obtaining accurate information, Patterson had seen a journal (which he'd later lost) of one of the passengers. He also had "expiscated," in his word, old residents who might conceivably have information and found that two passengers, Alexander Cameron from Loch Broom on Scotland's west coast and Alexander Fraser of Beauly in the east, had witnessed the massacre at Culloden in April 1746, which hastened the collapse of the old Highland way of life and led to mass emigration. They had been eighteen years old at the time and lived to old age, which made them prime subjects for my book. Another *Hector* passenger came to vivid life through the discovery of a big copper-coloured key among archival artifacts. It seems that the key

For PICTOU HARBOUR in NOVA SCOTIA, BOSTON and FAL-MOUTH in NEW ENGLAND.

THE SHIP HECTOR, JOHN SPEIR mafter, burthen 200 tons, now lying in the harbour of GREE-NOCK. For freight or paffage apply to John Pagan merchant in Glaf-gow, Lee, Tucker, and Co. merchants in Gree-nock; and in order to accommodate all paffengers that may offer, the fhip will wait until the 10th of May next, but will pofitively fail betwixt and the 15th of that month.

N.B. Pictou harbour lyes directly oppofite to the ifland of St. John's, at the diftance of 15 miles only.

The *Hector's* journey to Pictou began with ship-owner John Pagan's advertisment in the *Edinburgh Advertiser* in 1773, directed "To All Farmers and others in Scotland, who are inclined to settle upon easy terms in the Province of Nova Scotia in North America."

had been brought to Pictou by a hot-tempered young blacksmith named Roderick "Rory" MacKay of Beauly, who used it to escape from Inverness jail before joining the *Hector* at Loch Broom before it sailed for Pictou.

Thus one by one the people of the *Hector* came into focus but there was so little in Patterson's book about their lives before they took ship that I flew to the Highlands to fill the gaps. Starting at the Scottish Records Office in Edinburgh, I visited Loch Broom and Beauly, where *Hector* people had lived, and the cenotaph at Culloden, where the clan system died. After that terrible battle Jacobite estates were seized, chieftains stripped of power, kilt and tartan banned. Clansmen became prey to land owners who found they could make more money raising sheep than renting land to subsistence farmers. Thousands left for North America, seventy shiploads in 1770-1772, but nothing equalled 1773, the year the *Hector* sailed to Pictou. Dr. Samuel Johnson, riding a horse through the Highlands in September, called 1773 "an epidemical fury of emigration."

After two stormy months crossing the Atlantic the *Hector* arrived at a clearing in the woods on September 15. The passengers felt they had been deceived, for instead of the arable land promised they found virgin forest. It was too late in the year to plant crops and had it not been for friendly Mi'kmaq and the few settlers from New England who had preceded them to Pictou, they might have starved that first winter. They persisted and were the seed of the flowering of a New Scotland.

Scotland Farewell since its publication has had a life of its own. It was lifted off the printed page and transmuted into virtual reality when the town of Pictou built a museum and interpretative centre on Hector Quay with life-like figures of crew and passengers and lines from the book on the walls. Two marine architects were sent to Europe to search for records of the original *Hector*, two centuries after it had gone to the breaker's yard, and twenty years after the book was published a replica of the long-lost *Hector* was launched in Pictou Harbour on September 17, 2000. Among the 15,000 gathered to witness the event, twenty clans were represented.

15

THE SEARCH FOR OTHERNESS

"One of the pleasantest things in the world is going on a journey," wrote William Hazlitt. "Out of my country and out of myself I go," he sang, and left England in 1832 on a tour that required neither passport nor visa though there were brigands on the roads and bedbugs at the inns.

Had Hazlitt lived in the 20th century, the most warlike and destructive hundred-year period in history, the famous essayist might have been less carefree. By mid-century Evelyn Waugh was already claiming that the salad days of travel were over. "Never again, perhaps," he wrote in his retrospective *When the Going Was Good,* "shall we land on foreign soil with letter of credit and passport ... and feel the world wide open before us." But Waugh, who maintained he was a "traveller" rather than a "tourist," reckoned without the surge in mass travel two decades later: the travel agencies, group tours, jet aircraft and cruise ships that encouraged people to travel who had never travelled before.

Despite mounting anxieties and disappointments, millions of us board aircraft bound for destinations the Greeks call *Heterotopias,* "distant places of otherness far removed from our normal lives." Although more people are going more places, though wars and rumours of wars have shut down travel in countries stretching from the Congo to the Holy Land and into the Hindu Kush, in places still free from overt menace the tourist industry is busily denaturing the foreign and the authentic and offering us Big Macs, Coke, CNN and reruns of American TV. In one of the most exotic neighbourhoods I know, the Djemaa el Fna of Marrakech, which erupts

Seeking *Heterotopias* on the *Friendship Rose* schooner sailing out of St. Vincent. From Cuba down through the Windwards, Leewards and west to the Lesser Antilles, each Caribbean island was unique though only a few miles might separate them.

nightly in a medieval carnival of drummers, acrobats, snake charmers and medicine men, the roofs sprout satellite dishes like mine at home in Nova Scotia.

*   *   *

In the early 1970s I visited Mao Zedong's chaotic Cultural Revolution and a more dramatic contrast to today's rich and confident industrial colossus is hard to imagine. China had been convulsed by six years of brutal social engineering in which millions of young Red Guards mindlessly carried out Mao's destructive wishes. In two thousand miles of travel by train, car and Ilyushin-18 turboprop aircraft, strange sights and sounds assailed me several times a day. In a country where I heard a mynah bird croak "Long live Chairman Mao," I heard that no one could own property, there were no private

Since 1959 when the *Globe and Mail* become the first western newspaper to open a Peking bureau, China had been partial to Canadian journalists. With American organizations like UPI unwelcome there, I travelled in 1972 with a document from a Canadian client.

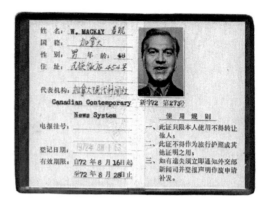

cars, no taxes, and a so-called hundred-year-old egg was preferred to a fresh egg.

The occasion was a trade delegation led by Minister of External Affairs Mitchell Sharp, Canada having become one of the first capitalist nations to establish diplomatic relations with the People's Republic. Although the Communists had banned American journalists, they permitted Canadian journalists to accompany the delegation, so I went somewhat deviously as a representative of one of UPI's Canadian clients. Thus on the sweltering morning of August 14, 1972, twenty-three years after the Communist Party seized control of the civil-war-torn nation, we flew into Canton (Guangzhou) from Vancouver in the *Empress of Lisbon,* a chartered CPR jet. According to my notes, "The pilot says we are the first plane from a non-communist country to land since 1949. Everyone is crowding the portholes. Paddy fields glint like green mirrors, water buffalo, red earth, people in white shirts and conical hats gazing up. Pearl River full of sampans, junks and ocean freighters."

On the tarmac we were met by a fleet of black cars and bossy young "Mr. Mao," our chief minder from the foreign ministry, and driven into Canton along avenues of semi-tropical red flowers and dirty grey and brown 19th-century warehouses and factories. There were a few ancient trucks but thousands of Shanghai-made bicycles, heavily laden with farm produce, coal, bricks and wood. There was a sweet and sour smell of cooking spices, charcoal, tobacco and brown coal smoke. We were taken to the Friendship Guest House in a compound formerly owned by a warlord where my old-fashioned room of dark wood contained a mosquito net, cigarettes, a thermos of tea, candies and two bottles of Chinese beer.

Our guides told us of the days when China was controlled by Westerners and signs in the Foreign Concession said "No Dogs No Chinese." In the Park of the People we had our first encounter with the legend of Doctor Norman Bethune from Gravenhurst, Ontario, whose dedication to the Communist cause in establishing hospitals and mobile medical units during the Sino-Japanese war was to influence Communist China's attitudes toward Canada for decades. Bethune died in China in November 1939 from blood poisoning contracted while operating on a wounded soldier. Mao, apparently deeply moved by Bethune's dedication, perhaps also because a Canadian doctor was useful agit-prop, wrote a glowing tribute and circu-

lated it to Chinese schools. "We must all learn the spirit of absolute selflessness from him," Mao wrote. "A person's ability may be great or small, but if he/she has this spirit, he/she is already no-

Little known in Canada, Dr. Norman Bethune of Gravenhurst, Ontario, was an iconic hero in Communist China, a surgeon in Mao's People's Army, where he lost his life during the Sino-Japanese war of 1938-39.

ble-minded and pure, a person of moral integrity and above vulgar interests, a person of value to the people." There are Bethune statues, a pavilion, a museum, school and hospital in China, and his remains lie in the Revolutionary Martyrs' Cemetery, which we duly visited in the busy industrial northern city of Shijiazhuang, capital of Hebei province.

Reporting on China entailed the task of correcting western misapprehensions that did not fit the facts. The legendary Barefoot Doctors of the Cultural Revolution, for example, turned out to be quite ordinary cheerful, efficient young men and women who wore shoes or sandals like everyone else and had responsibilities similar, in a nation short of physicians, to Canada's nurse-practitioners. As well as attending to ailments they dispensed medicines and contraceptives and biked among the villages teaching hygiene and birth control.

Having read in American medical journals that acupuncture as the sole anesthetic for brain surgery was useless, I attended an operation in Canton's Chung Shan Hospital where twenty-four-year-old Chen Yueh Hua, a small-boned, boyish-looking farmer, told us he had fallen off a bamboo staging and fractured his skull. Dr. Kao Shung Kahn, assistant chief surgeon, said the fracture was causing pressure on Chen's brain and a broken bone had to be replaced by a plastic plate.

We watched the procedure from an observation booth one morning in a dark and dingy cement-walled operating room of doubtful hygiene. Doctors inserted acupuncture needles as Chen lay on the operating table waiting for them to block off nerves that carry pain. There were conventional anesthetics on hand but apparently they were not needed. After the last stitch was sewn into Chen's scalp the patient slowly sat up. He looked dazed but smiling and was helped onto a gurney and wheeled to where we reporters were waiting. He told us he had felt a jolting sensation but no pain. I would have liked to know how he fared later.

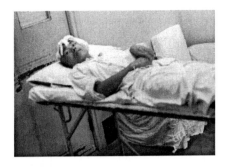

Chen Yueh Hua talks to Canadian journalists minutes after surgery for a skull injury carried out solely with acupuncture anesthetic.

Before the massive migration to cities of later years, at least 80 per cent of the population worked on the land and we were driven several miles into the lush countryside to a model rice plantation, the Tal Nan People's Commune, a huge stretch of flat fertile land with its own hospital, machine shop, cement factory, rice polishing factory and coal mine for smelting iron. We met a thirty-four-year-old farmer named Chen Peng Chun, a lean smiling man in shorts, white shirt and sandals, who invited us into his four-room home to meet his wife and five-year-old son and eight-year-old daughter. His father had been a poor labourer for a landlord before the Communists came to power, he said. "There was never enough to eat. We sometimes had to exist on sweet potatoes and wild herbs. Now everyone has medical care and enough to eat. There is no more selling of children as there was before Liberation."

Chen and his wife owned a pig and eight chickens and worked in the communal paddies six days a week. They had noodles and tea for breakfast, a lunch of rice "and sometimes meat," and rice in the evening. Chen, I imagine, had been especially chosen to meet the foreign press and we were unable to get information about once-prosperous families, and there must have been many, who lost property and livelihood, and perhaps their lives, when the Communists took power.

When my hosts offered me a car, driver and translator for a small fee, I skipped the trade fair and went touring with notebook, tape

recorder and camera. Driving in the hills east of Canton one afternoon we came across an odd sight – an open lean-to containing a
great pile of rubber boots but no sign of water. They belonged to
the Lo Kong Commune, where we found eighteen girls between
seventeen and twenty-one, the March 8th Production Team founded
"In Honour of International Women's Liberation Day." Led by Yen
Wen Lan, a Canton high school graduate, the girls were part of a
gang working around the clock with hand tools and dynamite to
tunnel through a hill to provide water for a 2,000-acre tea plantation. The girls were the day shift – the other shifts were men and
boys – and in teams of six they sang work songs and laboured with
sledge hammers and big cold chisels; they had been working for a
year and would finish the last 200 feet during the next four months.
Their primitive hard hats were of heavy straw and they worked four
days a week in six inches of water in the ill-lit tunnel and slept in

Trucks, like cars, were few in 1970s China where bicycles and tricycles like this
one bearing a load of bricks were the norm.

This section of the Great Wall north of Peking was wide enough for ten soldiers marching side by side. Watch towers and six-foot parapets of the ancient crenellated structure had recently been repaired with traditional materials.

a dormitory like a Girl Guide camp, with a "wall newspaper" on which they critiqued each other's failings. Since urban schools had long since closed and youngsters been sent into the country in their millions, I asked Yen Wen Len what she wanted to do, thinking she would wish to return home. "I would like to learn enough to be a supervisor here," she said.

Two days later I was in Shanghai, one of the great cities of the world in the 1920s and '30s but shabby and neglected in 1972. It still had the country's best shops and restaurants, however, and a big-city feel like lower east-side Manhattan. Number One Department Store, which was so big I got lost for an hour when I strayed from my minders into crowds of shoppers one night, reputedly served tens of thousands of customers a day. The large choice of goods was well displayed compared with stores in east European Communist countries, for China's policy, unlike Russia's heavy industry policy at a similar stage of development, was to raise living standards with light industry.

In Peking, as it was then called, we stayed at the Hotel of Nationalities and attended a formal banquet in the Great Hall of the People on Tiananmen Square. Mao had been ailing so our host was the moderate, charismatic Premier Zhou Enlai, co-founder of the Party and a cultivated Mandarin credited with restraining some of Mao's excesses and with setting China on its road to modernization. Zhou, who was seventy-four and would die of cancer within four years, greeted each of us warmly with a few words as we passed through the reception line. The banquet, which included bird's nest soup, demonstrated that at its best Chinese cuisine ranks with the best French and Italian. The only dish I could not bring myself to sample was sea slug, a cold, black rubbery two-inch blob which the locals seemed to enjoy. Beside each place were three glasses – an orange drink, a sweetish red wine and 80-proof *maotai*, the powerful white liquor made from sorghum, which some say tastes like paint thinner. During the many toasts I noticed the Chinese, unlike their guests, avoided *maotai* in favour of the harmless orange drink. Next day we walked off *maotai*'s effects by hiking a section of the Great Wall north of the capital.

I left China with a severe case of indigestion but with gratitude that I had seen the country before it became like the world's other

Premier Zhou Enlai, greeting Candian guests at a banquet in the Great Hall of China in 1972.

industrial giants, before Peking and Shanghai became modern cities of towering skyscrapers, shopping malls, traffic jams and multilane highways. I did, however get a vivid impression in 1972 of what this nation could do when it regained its ancient strength and confidence.

*   *   *

While living in London, Barbara and I found our *Heterotopia* in Spain's central Pyrenees, with the exhilaration of hiking the wild tangle of mountains, glaciers, alpine meadows and deep valleys along the French border between Pamplona and Andorra. The most savage of those peaks, inhabited by eagles, ibex and chamois, lay in the legendary Kingdom of Sobrarbe, which enfolds Ordesa National park and its twelve miles of canyon, woods and water as well as Val de Pineta, whose sheer cliffs stretch for miles into the high mountains.

The Sobrarbe extends about thirty miles from west of the village of Torla to the village of Venesque to the east and its three principal valleys run mostly south and north. Thus to travel from one valley into the other we had either to climb over a high shoulder of mountain or travel down the road for twenty-five miles to get around into the next valley. Map distances were deceptive. From Torla to Bielsa in the next big valley was maybe twenty miles as the eagle flies but it took us a day and a half to hike there on the steep stony mule tracks over the passes. Above us towered Pico del Inferno, Los Encantados, Maladettas and Monte Perdido. Although we never discovered why those snow-tipped peaks were "enchanted" or "accursed" or who had been lost on Monte Perdido, we were warned that getting lost could be as simple as wandering into a dead end of the wrong valley while following an elusive trail down from a mountain pass. Hilaire Belloc wrote in his 1923 book *The Pyrenees*, "It is more easy to die from exhaustion than in any other way in these hills" and suggested it was a good plan to carry rations for an extra day.

Weight was a constant problem, so our backpacks contained as little as possible: emergency rations of soup cubes, chocolate, trail mix, toilet paper, soap, binoculars, flashlight, compass, first aid, socks, underwear, a couple of paperback books, matches, maps, a little pan, knife, spoon, rain gear, and light "space blankets," which looked and rattled like aluminum foil on the few nights we slept in high refuge huts. For lunch we carried bread, sausage, cheese, water and a leather canteen with a nozzle from which we could squirt red wine into our mouths. We would usually get down into a valley

In one of the last wilderness areas of Europe we walked four or five hours a day, descending into a valley before nightfall to the food, wine and comfort of a village inn. There were scattered refuge huts in the High Pyrenees but few people.

every evening, where we could sleep at a *fonda* and have a reviving gin and Coke, since they had no tonic, and a hot meal, almost invariably vermicelli soup, broiled mutton, rice and caramel pudding. Dinner, bed and breakfast averaged the equivalent of five Canadian dollars for each of us.

Our best meal was an unexpected hot lunch. With our friend Greg Jensen we had been climbing one morning from Torla, at the entrance to Ordesa Park, toward the high pass which leads into Cirque de Gavarnie, the famous semicircle of precipices on the French side of the border, when we were overtaken by a tremendous rainstorm. Having noted a place called Bujaruela on the map, we pushed on, cold and wet, in hope of shelter. An hour later, while debating whether to turn back, we came at last to an alpine meadow and four desolate stone houses in the lap of Monte Perdido. We thought the buildings were deserted until Greg noticed a wisp of smoke. A spry little man answered our knocks and invited us into a cavernous room in which a wood fire burned on a stone dais in the middle of the stone floor, its smoke escaping through a hole in the roof. The refuge was 200 years old and though June, the time we were there, was a quiet month, as many as forty slept there each night in August. He apologized that he had only eggs and quickly concocted in a huge pan over the open fire a monster *tortilla de patatas* – eggs, chopped onions, potatoes and herbs – served with homemade bread and a red wine that looked almost black.

Belloc had written, "A Pyrenean path is the vaguest of things: it is a patch of trodden soil here and there, a few worn surfaces of rock, then perhaps a long stretch with no indication whatsoever." Perhaps trails had improved since his time, but any rate we luckily managed to avoid getting lost, though on one stormy evening near the high Pass of Sahun on the slopes of the Maladetas we were forced to take refuge in a woodcutter's empty bed, as in Goldilocks and the three bears. Greg Jensen, Barbara and I had been hiking from the beauti-

ful valley of Venasque to the village of Plan in the most remote valley in the 250-mile Pyrenean range, where the women still threshed
oats as their ancestors had for centuries, beating the stalks on slabs
of slate. During the afternoon, storm clouds had been massing over
the valleys and before dusk we crossed Sohun Pass into the sudden
full force of a driving rainstorm. We were wet through and with
miles still to go Barbara was feeling so ill and cold that her teeth were
chattering. We'd heard that people in risk of hypothermia must keep
moving, but as we hurried down the switchback trail we came upon
a providential lean-to with a big foam-rubber mattress piled with
blankets. No one was about so we got out of our wet clothes and
wrapped Barbara in blankets and lay on each side of her to keep her
warm. We were thus engaged when we heard a clanging mule bell
and two young woodcutters and a mule appeared at the open door.
They seemed friendly if confused, and they spoke a dialect we did
not understand, so never discovered how they felt about strangers in
their bed. Barbara was warmer by now and the rain had stopped so
we started to walk to Plan, and when we came to a logging road I
flagged down a vehicle which fortunately happened to be up there
that day. Greg and Barbara got in with our knapsacks and for reasons I cannot remember I walked the last five miles down into Plan.
As Barbara's diary recorded, "Sitting before a log fire in the kitchen
of the old *fonda* with coffee con leche and cognac, log fire in the
great fireplace, marvellous. Don came in wet from the last mile and a
half of his descent. A meal of potatoes, spinach, mutton grilled over
coals, feeling very good indeed."

How fine it was, as Hazlitt had written, "to come to some strag-
gling village, with the lights streaming through the surrounding
gloom."

During two other summers we walked a section of the eastern, or
Catalan, Pyrenees in the shadows of the Enchanted Mountains – the
Encantados – which had been more prosperous and more populated

in the Middle Ages. We began in the Val d'Aran, which looked and sounded, with its tinkling cow bells, like Switzerland. Connected to France by a tunnel and to the rest of Spain by the dizzying heights of the bare, lonely Bonaigua Pass, Val d'Aran contained quiet villages with medieval Romanesque churches, and forgotten little 17th-century spas, where wealthy Catalans came for the cure, like the one at the village of Arties where we discovered healing waters in the remains of a Roman bath dating from Hadrian's reign. After a typical day's hike of fourteen miles around Lake San Mauricio and the Parque of Agues Tortes, Barbara wrote, "We had a relaxing sulphur bath in two big lead tubs where the water was warm and soft and slightly gaseous and smelled a bit."

Otherness, by its very nature, must be a relative quality, and one person's exotic vacation spot is another's prosaic home, but for both of these the old ways were fading by the 1970s. Mountains that had been a virtually impassable wall, *una muralla rigido y apensas franqueable,* against invasive barbarians from the north and Moors from the south were no defence against Spanish modernity. Every summer we encountered more hydroelectric development, more tour buses and day trippers. Where there had been shepherds and lone hikers, there were omens of tourist business to come. In the "end of the world" mountain valleys around Salardú, Boi and Espot were turning into trendy ski resorts like those of the Alps.

16

ENCOUNTERS WITH RELIGION
AND ROYALTY

Two millennia before Alfred Hitchcock's 1940 movie *Foreign Correspondent* inspired me to dream of overseas assignments, Thucydides was sending news home from the Peloponnesian wars. It was only in 1802, however, that *The Times* of London instituted the modern practice of permanently basing reporters in far-flung places. By the end of the 19th century professional foreign correspondents had become media stars. Henry Morton Stanley had tracked down the elusive Dr. Livingston for the *New York Herald,* and dashing young Winston Churchill had covered the Boer War for the London *Morning Post.*

Foreign correspondents have followed a privileged trade with unusual access to important people and events, but unlike followers of proper professions – law or medicine – they observe no formal standards, sanctions or rules. Now in our TV and internet world of jet travel and failing newspapers, the old-time foreign correspondent is a dying breed, but I know of no other occupation which would have paid me to travel to exotic places, walk with kings, dine off bird's nest soup with Premier Zhou Enlai in Beijing and seek words from the lips of the famous, whether saintly, kingly or secular.

During most of the 20th century, Dr. Albert Schweitzer was our worldly embodiment of a Christ-like dedicated life. His credo, Reverence for Life, in which all sentient living things are capable of well-being, fear and pain and deserve our consideration, had left a deep impression when I read it at the age of eighteen. The idea of our clever human species, the outcome of three or four billion years of Darwinian selection, arrogantly killing less fortunate flesh and blood creatures for pleasure and calling it sport, stood starkly revealed as iniquitous.

A celebrated organist, Bach interpreter, philosopher, theologian, friend of Einstein, author, physician and surgeon, Dr. Schweitzer at the age of thirty-eight in 1913 had famously abandoned a brilliant career in Strasbourg to become a Protestant medical missionary in one of the hottest, wettest and unrewarding backwaters in equatorial Africa. North of the Congo and 800 miles up the Ogowe River near the town of Lambaréné

Physician, theologian, organist, missionary, Nobel laureate, author, Dr. Albert Schweitzer's books ranged from a life of Jesus to a treatise on organ construction. John F. Kennedy called him "one of the transcendent moral influences of our century."

in Gabon he founded a primitive hospital that grew into a village of healing with seventy corrugated iron and wooden huts, some of which he built himself, and 500 patients, including 250 lepers. By day he administered the native hospital of which he was pastor, chief physician and surgeon with a team of three younger doctors and ten nurses. At night by the light of kerosene lamps he wrote books on history, music and religion, dying there at the age of ninety.

I met this supernaturally gifted man in the autumn of 1954 on the ship taking him and his wife, Helene Bresslau, from Africa to Oslo to accept the Nobel Peace Prize, which he had won the previous year. At the age of seventy-nine, Schweitzer was big, craggy and imposing, in rumpled white drill suit, thick glasses and walrus moustache. He might have been an old-fashioned Alsatian farmer and did not seem particularly saintly. As we talked on the deck of the little ship about his campaign to stop nuclear testing, Dr. Schweitzer made sly Germanic jokes to two of his elderly female nursing staff about the rude antics three pet chimpanzees were performing in the ship's rigging.

I was intrigued to learn that this famous Christian humanist was a cousin of the existentialist Jean-Paul Sartre, for I could not imagine two men less alike. He assured me that they were on good terms but never discussed philosophy. "Love forgives everything," he said. "A new spirit must be born if we are to continue to exist after all the terrible things mankind has done and experienced." He told me he would use his $33,000 Nobel prize to develop a leprosarium and when I mentioned American supporters who had visited his outpost hospital and complained of a startling lack of common hygiene, he replied that modern American medicine would be useless in a jungle where patients must return to live in remote and unhygienic villages.

Meeting a legend can be disappointing and in Dr. Schweitzer I'd met a man whose life, for all its inspiring dedication to healing, had raised questions as to whether his sacrifice had been worthy of his genius; whether he had best served the modern world by shutting himself away for two thirds of his life in a remote jungle where he devoted himself to activities lesser men might have carried out more efficiently. Some had actually done better, I felt, such as Dr. Sidney Gilchrist's Canadian United Church medical mission at Dondi in Angola. But as I said goodbye to Dr. Schweitzer I thought of how this gifted man – author of *The Mystery of the Kingdom of God* and *The Quest for the Historical Jesus* – had created not only a primitive jungle hospital of wooden huts with no running water serving a few hundred leprous Africans but a role model for millions of people around the world with his sacrificial pursuit of a Christian ideal.

Two years earlier, while reporting on the 35th International

Eucharist Congress in Barcelona in May 1952, I encountered a more worldly saint. Cardinal Pierre-Marie Gerlier, Archbishop of Lyon, had been a soldier and lawyer, a liberal humanist who championed the left-wing "worker priest" movement and protected French Jews from the Nazis. Before becoming a priest he had been wounded and imprisoned in World War I. Attracting tens of thousands of Roman Catholics from around the world, this was the first such Congress since the war, its theme "the Eucharist saves the world," its aim to explain how God could exist amid war and holocaust. The Eucharist, the Cardinal said, was the remedy and corrective to the divergent and quarrelsome ideologies heaped on the Christian faith since Christ was adopted by the Roman Empire. There were conferences, expositions, medieval processions and a ceremony in the Olympic Stadium in which 840 priests stood before twenty-eight altars in the biggest ordination in history. It was a dazzling multi-ring affair, highlighted for me by the seventy-two-year-old Cardinal's lectures and his efforts to reunite the Catholic and Protestant faiths. Moved by the drama and grandeur of the celebrations and Gerlier's dream of a peaceable future among the world's warring faiths, for the only time in my life I had a strong if momentary impulse to join an organized religion. Though Charles Darwin had demolished the ancient universe, though God remained unknowable, though immortality still seemed impossible, the faith shown in Barcelona that spring reminded me that religion could be more than simply society's safety net and social glue.

I encountered religious people in many guises, but recall few more modest than Tenzing Norgay. A small, lithe brown man with a ready smile, Tenzing was in London on a rare visit from the Himalayan Mountaineering Institute in Darjeeling. He looked younger than his fifty-one years though a decade had passed since he and the New Zealand bee-keeper Edmund Hillary had become the first to conquer Mount Everest in May 1953. Lionized by the world, and above all in his country of Nepal, the impression he gave was one of quiet confidence and humour.

Born in Tibet to a poor Sherpa family, he was taken as a child to the Rongbuk Buddhist monastery in the shadow of Everest, where a holy man predicted he would achieve great things and said his name meant "Wealthy Fortunate Follower of Religion." That the conquest of Everest, or Chomolungma as Sherpas call it, had a religious aspect had not occurred to me until he said he left an offering to the gods in the snow when he reached the top of the mountain, which his people believe sacred.

Tenzing had been climbing on Everest since 1935 and had made half a dozen failed attempts on the summit, including an ill-fated effort in the spring of 1947 with an obsessive, poorly-equipped Canadian with little experience. From the shadow of the monastery where Tenzing had received his name, he and another Sherpa and Earl Denman from British Columbia were turned back by the elements and lack of funding and preparation. After Tenzing's death in Darjeeling at the age of seventy-four, a member of the British Everest Expedition recalled, "His head might have been turned by the godlike adulation he received after the climb but his innate strength of character, and his flashing smile, pulled him through."

*   *   *

The royalty I encountered in Lisbon's garden suburb of Estoril appeared to have accepted their exile quietly, pleased perhaps that the world remembered them at all. Tall, balding Umberto II of Italy, who occupied the throne for only a month in 1946, recalled how his grandfather had created Italy like a jigsaw puzzle out of small states. Umberto lived in an unpretentious seaside villa with his wife, son and three daughters, barred from Italy by a republican constitution. While strolling in his garden he told me that should the people of Italy so wish he would like to return; meantime he was studying the history of the House of Savoy and his hobby was mountain climbing.

Also in Estoril was the Bourbon Pretender, Henri, Count of Paris, who lived in a rambling farm house with his wife and eleven children and published the family journal *Nous onze* while longing for Paris. The Portuguese Pretender, Duarte Nuno, had recently been allowed to return, but Portugal had been a republic for so long that attempts to restore the monarchy had failed. An oddity in Estoril's royal mile was the former Hungarian Regent, Admiral Nicholas Horthy, the last commander of the Austro-Hungarian navy and aide-de-camp to Emperor Franz Josef. He had become regent in 1920 when that landlocked country had neither king nor navy. An extreme right-wing authoritarian who consorted with Hitler and Mussolini, he had turned against Hitler when he realized the Allies were winning. Imprisoned by the Nazis, rescued by Americans, he appeared for the prosecution at the Nuremberg trials and found refuge in Salazar's Portugal, where he wrote *My Life for Hungary*, the story of the last of the Axis leaders of World War II. Now in his eighties, he sometimes appeared with his wife at American and British embassy receptions.

My favourite was Don Juan, Count of Barcelona, veteran of the British navy and, like his Estoril neighbour King Carol of Romania, a great grandson of Queen Victoria and second cousin of England's King George VI. The son of King Alfonso XIII, exiled in 1910, Juan Carlos Teresa Silvestre Alfonso de Borbón y Battenberg had a seaman's tattoo and an easy manner. Living at Villa Giralda, he kept a low profile but appeared at embassy cocktail parties given by General Francisco Franco's affable little brother Nicholas, ambassador to Portugal, whom we called Nicky. Don Juan obviously disliked Francisco Franco and wanted a liberal constitutional monarchy. Francisco Franco, who, unlike the tall, manly Don Juan, was small and fat and personally unimposing, had other ideas and was arrang-

In the final years of Franco's regime, the only Spaniards opposing Don Juan were General Franco, the fascist Falange movement and the police. The Church, industrialists, the middle and working classes, all supported the popular Pretender though it would be his son who inherited the throne.

ing for Don Juan's elder son to take the throne, mistakenly thinking young Juan Carlos less liberal than this father.

The saddest story I was called upon to report during my four years in Portugal concerned Don Juan's family in January 1956. The eighteen-year-old Juan Carlos, back from military college in Spain for the Christmas holidays, was at home with his fifteen-year-old brother Alfonso examining a new revolver when it accidentally discharged and killed Alfonso. There were inevitable rumours about who was actually holding the gun at the time, but the official communiqué was clear: "While His Highness Prince Alfonso was cleaning a revolver last evening with his brother, a shot was fired hitting his forehead and killing him in a few minutes."

Assuming the throne in 1975 after Franco's death, King Juan Carlos assured Spain's successful transition from feudal dictatorship to modern parliamentary democracy.

17

OLD IRELAND

The sun bright on the Irish Sea and Celtic music jigging from our ship's radio, in 1945 I had my first glimpse of Ireland. Wartime convoys usually kept well clear of the Republic, whose ambiguous neutrality had denied the Allies a precious haven from Nazi U-boats, but on this calm Sunday morning toward the end of the war we were close enough to see silent white cottages, farms, fields, the steeples of a town. I imagined church bells and peat smoke. Ireland had become so isolated – the Dublin government euphemistically called World War II "the emergency" – the country seemed alien and mysterious. I thought of people eating breakfast and preparing for Mass and wondered what they were like, having no idea that fifty years later I would actually be living among them in the very county I now was looking at. After a while I went down to breakfast as *Peik* steamed her steady twelve knots up the Irish Sea to Liverpool and Scotland to deliver our cargo of American bunker oil.

Eighteen years were to pass before I set foot on Irish soil, when on June 26, 1963, I flew from London with Barbara to report on John F. Kennedy's ceremonial visit to the land of his ancestors. The young President met his Fitzgerald kinfolk in County Limerick, was made Freeman of Wexford Town, met third cousin Mary Kennedy Ryan and drank tea in the Dungenstown, County Wexford, cottage of his great grandfather Patrick Kennedy, farmer and cooper, who emigrated to Boston in "Black 1847," the worst year of the Great Famine. "This," said JFK, "is where it all began."

In Dublin Kennedy joined Ireland's New York-born President Éamon de Valera to launch the American Irish Foundation, plant

Neat as a yacht cabin and weighing three quarters of a ton, our horse-drawn caravan accommodated four people, with gas stove, folding bunks, shelves and drawers. In exchange for harnessing, feeding and grooming, Prince hauled us an average of ten miles a day with few complaints.

the obligatory tree and receive an Irish coat of arms. It was only long after the visit that authorities released the chilling news that Kennedy had received three Irish death threats. It had been expected Kennedy would "do big things for Ireland," but after his assassination in Texas five months later it was left to American private investment to fuel Ireland's astonishing economic surge in the 1990s and help create *an Tíogar Ceilteach,* the so-called Celtic Tiger.

In August 1964 Barbara, Marina and Karen, then aged ten and eight, travelled with me by plane, train and bus from London to Kenmare in County Kerry, where we hired a horse-drawn caravan like those once used by Tinkers, who nowadays travel in cars and vans. Our red, white, blue and yellow wood-panelled wagon was twelve feet long, not counting the shafts, and equipped with bunks, a tiny kitchen, automobile tires and a massive brake for the steep hills. Our world-weary brown gelding, Prince, who had a white star on his forehead, was justifiably suspicious. The last time I'd driven a horse I was nine years old on a hay rake at Grand Pré near Wolfville, so I had a lot to learn, including the Irish terms *Wee!* for Whoa, and

Go way! for Giddiup. Thankfully the roads were empty but they were very, very narrow.

Each morning after breakfast we sallied forth with rope and halter and a bucket of oats in the pasture where we'd spent the night. Our challenge was to persuade Prince to accept his bridle and then back into the shafts without getting tangled in his harness. We had to remember to attach trace chains to his collar hooks so he could pull the contraption, and to his breeching straps so the wagon wouldn't bump his rump. Then we were off, after paying the farmer a shilling for the hospitality of his field. We weren't always welcome. Having been on the road a week, burnt by sun and wind, scruffy and smelly with no place to wash, we came to a farm where a woman took a look at our gypsy wagon and ordered her children into the house. It took a while to convince her we had no desire to steal her children, having two of our own.

From the market town of Kenmare on the borders of Kerry and Cork we trekked west down Kenmare Bay to the Beara Peninsula, one of the five thick fingers which point to Canada. There were vistas of mountainous MacGillikuddy Reeks to the north, Cahas to the south, and in the village of Ardgroom a prehistoric stone circle that we were told was a calendar. Further on, the village of Eyries was out of a twee Disney film: four fancy pubs, pastel houses and the world's biggest Ogham Stone from the 5th century. Like the Ring of Kerry up the coast, the Ring of Beara is a land of mountains, empty beaches, cliffs, bogs, moors, waterfalls, forts, castles, tombs and stone circles built in 2500 BC. Beara, we were told, was a Spanish princess who married the well-travelled Eoin Mor, 2nd-century King of Munster, and was not to be confused with An Cailech Beara, The Old Hag of Beara, an ancient personification of raw Nature. An Cailech, they say, transformed herself into the unusual slab of stone which stands on the shore to this day. Why she would want to do such a thing was not explained.

Our average speed was three miles an hour. Like turtles we were part of the landscape as we logged our ten miles a day, except, that is, for the day we got stuck. We were coming down a narrow mountain road when our right front wheel got jammed into a deep cut in the solid rock. We tried pulling and pushing until old Prince, exasperated, refused to pull any more. There was no one about, no traffic, no houses. We unhitched Prince, gave him his oat bag and as time passed and rain threatened we were wondering what to do next when four men popped out of the fields. From afar they seemed formally dressed as for the office, but as they drew close we saw their suit coats were shabby hand-me-downs, their white shirts grubby and mended, their boots muddy, the uniform of field workers. They were chatty and promising but it became clear that each had a different idea of how to proceed and there seemed to be no Irish words for yes and no. One man wandered off to find a rope, another to borrow a donkey, but when they returned Prince began to take an interest again and with him pulling and the rest of us pushing and lifting and many strained mentions of Jesus, Mary and Joseph, we got the wagon free with nothing lost except two broken dishes and Prince's confidence in the driver. Next morning Prince stamped on my toes while I was trying to put on his halter and drove my boot deep into the bog, which mercifully was soft and mushy.

At the village of Adrigole, overlooked by Hungry Hill and Mares Tail waterfall, we parked at the top of a meadow which sloped steeply down to a small sandy beach on Bantry Bay. Children not being great lovers of scenery, we were pleased that Marina and Karen, who had been concealing their boredom behind comic books, were making new friends and heading for the beach in their swimsuits. The little beach looked safe, the farmer's children were older than ours and appeared responsible, so I retired to our caravan and picked up a book. Barbara had borrowed a bike and pedalled off to shop for our dinner in the village. Every so often I glanced down the hill where the children were splashing about. The day was hot and humid. I don't know how long I slept, probably less than ten minutes, but I snapped awake with a chill feeling that something was wrong.

I pulled on my boots and tumbled out of the caravan to see Karen bobbing and struggling in the incoming tide and Marina and the farm children trying vainly to pull her to safety. I was already running down the field when I saw Karen go under, but managed to reach her before she went down again. Getting us both back to firm land was difficult. Whenever I tried to find my footing the sand fell away and plunged us back into deep water. I'm sure there was talk of divine intervention in the village that night, but with Karen safely sleeping in the caravan I recalled that flood tides are often accompanied by a freshening breeze of the sort that mercifully woke me up.

Back on the road, two days and eighteen miles later we raised Glengariff, a lush green tourist town in a valley of crags and glens and semi-tropical gardens sweetened by the Gulf Stream; once a popular Victorian resort, it was favoured by Wordsworth and Thackeray. Rolling into Glengariff on a Saturday evening, Prince took it into his head to break unbidden into a brisk trot. Since I had been walking beside the wagon, as I had for most of our hundred-mile trek to spare him my 175 pounds, I was obliged to run with him. Soon Barbara and the children were down from the wagon and running too. Unused to such fun, Prince threw his hind right shoe as we went careening down the main street, pots and pans and dishes clattering, everybody in high spirits, onlookers cheering, and Prince's remaining shoes striking sparks off the dark road. We found a blacksmith and spent the night in a field on the edge of town. Sunday morning we awoke to a little man sitting on a boulder and playing a tin whistle. Leaving Glengariff we had to restrain Prince from cantering all the way to his stable in Kenmare through the damp and echoing tunnel that connects Cork with Kerry under the mountains.

Kenmare with its modern arts and crafts and tourist restaurants is described in current guidebooks as "the Jewel in the Ring of Kerry," but in this valley in 1846 thousands of men women and children died of starvation and disease in the Great Famine. "Kenmare was completely paralyzed," wrote William Steuart Trench, estate manager for Lord Lansdowne. "People succumbed to their fate almost without a struggle. They died on the roads, they died in the fields, they died in the mountain." Trench convinced Lord Lansdowne it would be cheaper to pay the fares to Quebec of 3,500 starving tenants than feed them at home and the great escape to Canada began. In the following year 100,000 Irish embarked for Canada as if fleeing from war.

During the 1960s I returned to Ireland to help friends restore 16th-century Leamcon House in County Cork, where the fields are checkered in half a dozen shades of green and hedgerows bloom with pink honeysuckle and purple fuschia like Chinese lanterns. At the village of Ballydehob, Nell and Julia, two indomitable old sisters, sold us bacon, eggs, bread, tinned custard, potatoes and peat from a counter in a corner of their busy little pub when they weren't pouring beer. Leamcon House, a grey stone mansion on a bare Atlantic headland overlooking Roaring Water Bay, was built by the Elizabethan English colonists known as planters on land seized from the Irish. In more recent times Tinkers, or Travellers, the gypsy-like Irish whose ancestors were uprooted during the Great Famine and earlier calamities, were said to have been camping there. The broken floors were perilous, the fireplaces walled up, the roof leaked, and there was neither electricity nor running water.

I was working alone on repairs there one week when a red-haired Traveller selling potatoes and coal out of a battered black van suggested the little bones I found while unblocking a fireplace were the bones of dead babies. I scoffed, but although Leamcon's only close neighbour was an empty ruin of a medieval castle I was awakened one night soon after by a baby's cries. My bed being temporarily perched

A wonder of nature and one of the spectacular views in the west of Ireland, the cliffs of Mohr in County Clare rise 700 feet above the Atlantic.

on loose boards with gaps between, I dared not risk getting up in the dark for fear of falling through the floor, so I cursed the power of suggestion in this country of banshees and pookas and struggled back to sleep. Next morning, a lovely sunny day, I was fetching tools from the basement when I met a little ginger cat which commenced the hungry feral cries of a phantom baby.

Throughout the 1960s and '70s we roamed the haunted landscapes of the west from Donegal down through the stony beauty of Connemara to the stark hills and megalithic tombs of the Burren of Clare and Great Blasket Island in Dingle Bay, reached in a rubber dinghy from the fishing village of Dunquin, where the movie *Ryan's Daughter* was filmed. Where once there had been hundreds of people living above its stark cliffs in thirty rough stone houses, fishing, growing oats in the sandy soil and keeping a few cows, there was only the wind, the holly, goat willow and the rabbits.

Unless you happened to be a poor tenant farmer, the west with its stunning vistas, silent mountains, sea cliffs, ruined castles, empty roads and Gaelic otherness, could be intensely seductive. But behind the touristic allure and lively *"craic"* or pub chatter, what came to be called "the great silence" haunted the depopulated landscape. Virtually the only memorials we saw were overgrown graves and tumbled, moss-covered stones where cottages and villages had been. I had not been there long when I began to notice that no one spoke of the 19th-century potato famine that had done the country such damage.

Due to the mysterious *Phytophthora infestans,* brought to Europe by ship, apparently from Canada and the eastern U.S., Ireland's food supply decreased by 30 per cent and in the rural west the poor were reduced to eating nettles, seaweed, stolen turnips and baked hedgehogs until by the autumn of 1846 death appeared as "famine fever" or typhus and dysentery. The semi-official *Times* of London called it an act of God, though the victims blamed English absentee landlords, cruel rents, evictions, racism, lack of official compassion, the stupidity of a monoculture, the unregulated trade in which grain was shipped to England from the richer fields of eastern Ireland. In the decade 1845-1855 it has been estimated that two million people, a third of the population, fled to Britain, or America and Canada or simply died of "famine fever." The Republic became more Roman Catholic than it had been – "the Pope's last bastion" – exporting faith as well as people. At one time, it was said, a third of the world's Catholic bishops were Irish.

For generations after the Famine, peasants in the west of Ireland were said to be of two classes, "the poor and the destitute." By the 1960s, however, the people who had been conquered by the British in Elizabethan times had been self-governing for a generation and rural poverty and drudgery were receding before our eyes as we travelled the byroads of the west. Given the fatal errors and omissions of the British, the inevitable question no one we met seemed to ask was whether the Potato Famine might have been much less lethal – or indeed not have happened at all – if the Irish had been free to rule themselves in the 19th century.

The mass grave of nine thousand famine victims in Skibbereen, County Cork. The plaque reads, "In memory of the victims of the Famine 1845-48 whose coffinless bodies were buried in this plot."

In whitewashed kitchens with their "dressers" for cups and dishes and pictures of the Pope, the Virgin and the Sacred Heart, stoves and electricity were replacing open hearths and oil lamps, though out in the fields men worked with scythe and sickle, harvested peat with slane and pike and carried it home in crill baskets on donkeys.

"A hard life? By God, it was, the hardest," said a bachelor farmer in Ballydehob. "Before the machines came the lads done everything with their hands and muscles but somehow people seemed happier then." Nor had they lost their sense of humour, for a sign at one of the traditional pubs whose landlords doubled as undertakers, said, "Why lead a miserable life when you can be decently buried for seven pounds." Rural social life meant Mass, the village pub and *Ceili* bands in the "ballrooms of romance," drafty, ill-lit community halls, a far cry from Éamon de Valera's oft-quoted vision of "comely maidens dancing at the crossroads."

At Barbara's suggestion I began research, in Canada and Ireland, on *Flight from Famine: The Coming of the Irish to Canada*, which was published in 1990. The reluctance to talk about the Famine which I encountered in Ireland right up to the 1990s was not fully overcome

In Black '47, the worst year of the famine, 100,000 Irish embarked for Canada as if fleeing from a war.

....

until 1995, the eve of the famine's 150th anniversary, when President Mary Robinson spoke in Dáil Éireann, the lower house of parliament, of the need of Irish everywhere to commemorate the Famine and the diaspora. Those who had been silent began to talk, scholarly researchers discovered hitherto unknown testimony and letters, and a spate of books, and monuments appeared all dedicated to *An Gorta Mór*, the Great Hunger.

Thousands had died on ill-founded "coffin ships" and were buried at sea; 11,543 men, women and children died in British North America, where most of the deaths were caused by typhus and other diseases in the quarantine stations of Grosse Isle, Quebec, and Partridge Island, New Brunswick, but thousands also died in Montreal, Kingston and Toronto. That the misery was concentrated in New Brunswick, Quebec and Upper Canada was largely due to the U.S. having imposed strict landing regulations so that the neediest and sickest had to go to the British colonies. In the following year Canada imposed similar restrictions.

They arrived when Canada was new and they were an ethnic group second in number only to the French, but accounts of the Gaelic Irish were scanty, compared with books about pioneer English and Scots. The printed sources were mainly two books that appeared some twenty years after the famine. In one of them, *The Irishman in Canada,* published in 1877 by Nicholas Flood Davin, a Limerick lawyer and journalist who emigrated to Toronto, the author described people in all walks of life who had contributed to the new country at a time when a quarter of all Canadians spoke with an Irish accent. "The Irishman has played so large a part in Canada," he wrote, "that his history could not be written without writing, to some extent, the history of Canada."

Barbara and I having learned to love Ireland, in the mid-1990s when she retired as associate vice-rector at Concordia University in Montreal, we moved to Ireland to be closer to Karen and Marina, who were living in London, and to our grandchildren, Marina's daughter Siân Lewis and son Matthew Lewis.

Our daughters, Karen (at left) and Marina in London.

18

THE CELTIC TIGER

In the summer of 1990 Barbara and I bought a farmhouse at the southeast corner of Ireland where the Atlantic meets the Irish Sea. Total strangers said "Welcome home," though we had no Irish roots and home was far away in Montreal. Pat, the shy old bachelor farmer who lived alone up the lane, left a basket of fresh eggs on our doorstep.

The lonely Atlantic beauty and fading Gaelic folkways of the west would naturally have been our first choice, but our visits had made us wary. "Soft morning," a Cork or Kerry person will tell you, whether in mist, drizzle or torrent, and we'd heard of the Americans who bought a small farm where it rained every day for a year until they left. Barbara, in Ireland in 1989 to address a family therapy conference, brought back enticing photos of County Wexford, which boasts the most sunshine in the country. Colonized by 12th century Anglo-Normans from Wales, the rich farm lands of County Wexford grow more wheat and sugar beet than potatoes, and though the Irish language may accompany English on road signs it is rarely spoken. In the Barony of Forth and Bargy, where we lived, there were remnants of an Old English dialect called Yola and neighbours had English names like Stafford, Shortall, Jeffers and Furlong though otherwise thoroughly Irish.

The house in Moortown Great (there was also Moortown Little) stood alone, gaunt and unloved, up a long lane bordered by wild hedges of white hawthorn, blackberry and orange montbresia. Though it was no dream house, our daughter Karen cast the deciding vote. "Buy it," she said. Quite coincidentally, this stretch of

The price was right, the façade newly-painted, and it stood in seductively solitary acres in Moortown Great amid the verdant and surprisingly sunny fields of south County Wexford, but it needed much work.

County Wexford had been the bit of Ireland I'd glimpsed from my ship forty-five years earlier during the war when I'd wondered about its people. Now I would find out.

Friends from Canada and England came expecting to find us in a town, but Moortown was neither town nor moor but what was called a town land, an ancient term for something smaller than a parish, and consisted of broad fields, lush meadows, shaggy trees, untended hedges. There were sheep, cattle and horses, gulls and crows and scattered white or pale yellow houses and two crossroads pubs. It was three miles as the gull flies from the Atlantic fishing village of Kilmore Quay and eight from Wexford Town, the county seat founded by 9th-century Danish Vikings who called it Weisfiord.

We paid the Irish equivalent of $50,000 for a century-old house which had started life as a farm labourer's state-subsidized four-room "two up and two down" with attached cattle shed. Over the years it had acquired electricity, a forty-nine-foot well, an indoor toilet which drained to a shallow cesspit unwisely sited ten feet from our front door, a battered peat-burning white stove to augment a fireplace, and a single-storey, flat-roofed 1960s addition containing a bathroom and small sitting room. The roof of quarried slate looked sound but we were apprehensive when we learned our walls were made of "random rubble," which turned out to be nothing worse than foot-thick masonry made of "stones of uneven size." The real hazards were the absence of damp-proofing in that wet country and the presence of ugly flammable compressed wood hopefully called "beauty board" which lined the walls of the primitive little kitchen.

The place was barely habitable, if you didn't mind camping among sickly green walls, but it cried out for renovation – walls, floors, wiring, plumbing, everything – and we wanted more space. Fortunately, Ireland at the time was a home-builder's theme park full of skilled, reliable men and Ballymitty Supply Stores two miles away was pleased to get our business. For renovations and additions we paid roughly the same amount we'd originally paid for the house itself, having bought it before the Celtic Tiger's labour shortages and inflation transformed Ireland from one of western Europe's poorest countries into, briefly, one of the richest and most expensive. What had not been apparent when we purchased the house was that Ireland was on the cusp of a dramatic revival.

Ireland's spectacular rebirth had been long coming. After freeing the Republic from Britain's domination the Prime Minister or *Taoiseach,* Éamon de Valera, had vainly sought national self-sufficiency through protectionism and antiquated farming. He was an iconic, controversial leader, revered for his fight for independence but criticized for holding the country back. I had interviewed him many years earlier in Lisbon when he visited Salazar, with whom, although he was no dictator, "Dev" shared ultra-conservative Catholic family values. At the age of seventy-five he might have been a farmer in his Sunday suit and boots as he expounded a romantic and unsustainable creed of old fashioned rural self-sufficiency.

"Dev" was elevated in 1959 to the largely-ceremonial post of

President, which allowed Prime Minister Seán Lemass to modernize farming and education and attract North American investment with subsidies and low taxes. In 1973 Ireland joined the European Economic Community, which transformed the country by subsidizing farmers, opening Continental markets, building motorways, overhauling the all-important tourist industry and inspiring social change. The Catholic Church lost much of the power it had held since the Great Famine. Nevertheless by the 1980s the country was plagued with overspending. Emigration was on the rise again, and with so many youngsters enjoying free education and then emigrating it was feared Ireland was educating its youth for the benefit of Britain, North America and Australia.

If you renovate a house in a foreign country, I discovered, you should stay in it. Otherwise you are inviting trouble. In the summer of 1991 Barbara and I returned to find the plumbing did not work. There was also a fishy smell that we thought came from the ancient fish-paste glue on the wall paper we'd been stripping, but searching for its source one night I happened to touch the kitchen wall. It seemed abnormally warm. The fuse box was so hot the old ceramic fuses were crumbling like stale cookies. I switched off the power and, fearing there were flames in the walls, hauled our mattress down the narrow stairs and we slept on the ground floor.

Next morning we received the sad news that Margaret, diagnosed with virulent cancer, had died with shocking suddenness in London. Margaret's brother Bob Anderson flew from Ontario and Karen, Marina, her husband Spencer Lewis, Barbara and I arranged a memorial service in Golders Green crematorium. The little chapel was crowded, there was no minister, Marina and I read poetry, and the music was the jazz Margaret loved. We placed a commemorative tree and a plaque in Bloomsbury's Tavistock Square which reads: "Guite MacKay (Margaret Anderson 1924-1991) A Canadian who loved London."

In our seventeen years together Margaret had enriched my life and brought joy to many. After her death I received a letter from our mutual friend, veteran CBC documentary-maker John David Hamilton, who had known Margaret since she worked as a nineteen-year-old junior at Canadian Press in New York. "I spent much of the night mourning Margaret," he wrote. "She had an intensity and warmth that were all her own."

Back in Moortown, Cissy Carty in her crossroads shop assured us she would send "a mighty man" to put our wiring and plumbing right. The man who knocked on our door next morning was short, dark, middle-aged, stocky, and though he did not strike us as mighty we discovered what Cissy meant. Dick Shortall was one of those talented if uncommon people who amply compensate for challenges in reading and writing. Dick was intelligent, creative, read schematic diagrams with speed and accuracy and had a solution for every problem. Raised in Kilkenny, Dick had fled from a harsh Christian Brothers school and picked up what further education he could in the London building trades. As lively as a leprechaun, Dick was a teetotaller amid boozers, a self-taught singer of sentimental songs with a powerful baritone that charmed pub-goers in three counties. He became our master builder and life-long friend.

Since we had to spend most of each year three thousand miles away in Montreal, a friend volunteered to be our locum. Norman

Kunlop, former seminarian, superb chef, amateur philosopher and renovator, had long wanted to visit Ireland

The ebullient Dick Shortall, a master builder, who came to help renovate and stayed to become a close friend, sharing "a cuppa" by the front door.

and was willing to supervise construction, buy supplies and act as paymaster in return for a rent-free six months. In one of life's unexpected serendipities, Norman took over in mid-November and was there when workmen hammered and drilled, compressors whined and winter winds and rain howled around boarded-up windows. At Christmas he bought a ten-speed bike, and since he had ruddy features and a white beard children called him Santa Claus as he whizzed around the country roads. People were still asking us about "Narman" years after he had left.

Thanks to the work of Dick and Norman, when Barbara and I returned in the spring of 1992 we had time to get to know our neighbours and to welcome family and friends from Canada and England. We explored medieval Cistercian abbeys, ruined castles of Kings Templar and Knights Hospitaller, miles of empty beaches and the 13th-century lighthouse on Hook Head. On the Saltee islands just off the coast we discovered a private principality invented by a romantic local businessman, Michael Neal, who purchased an uninhabited island in 1943, built a huge cement throne on a hillside and held his own coronation ceremony. When the British College of Arms refused to recognize him, Wexford County Council dubbed him "Prince Michael of the Saltees" and billed him for property taxes. Michael is dead along with his dream of turning his humpbacked island into an Irish Monte Carlo. It is now a bird sanctuary.

We improved the house, building a septic system to replace the cesspit outside the front door, and enlarged the grounds by buying the two-acre field next door, which required cutting a swath through an enormous wild hedge. Barbara planted birch, elm and conifer trees and created a perennial cottage garden with fuschia, ceanothis, lilies, honeysuckle, tulips, daffodils, gladioli, bachelor's buttons, evening-scented stock, bright orange and yellow mimula, poppies and chrysanthemums. Marina and Spencer, who lived in London, came with our grandchildren Siân and Matthew, as did Karen with

Grandchildren Siân and Matthew hunting Easter eggs at Moortown, where they frequently came to visit from their home in London.

her husband, Richard Jenner. Friends who had "always wanted" to come to Ireland found their motivation; fifty came in our bumper house guest summer of 1994.

Although some find it difficult to make new friends as they grow older, in Ireland it seemed easy to make friends both among the locals and the "folks from away" who restored traditional farmhouses for vacation or retirement, the farmers preferring to build dull, comfortable bungalows with their EU windfalls. We made friends too with descendants of the Protestant Ascendancy – now ruefully calling themselves the Descendancy – who live frugally in ancient drafty mansions and regard themselves as Irish though they speak upper-class English and retain strong ties with England. In one Ascendancy mansion, which was so run-down that small trees were sprouting from the roof, we found a portrait of the scourge of Ireland himself, Oliver Cromwell, hanging in the dining room.

Other neighbours were Nixy and Johnny the Blacksmith. Nixy, who planted an acre of potatoes in our field one year and had the special Irish flair for words, was a bachelor who lived with "the lads," who we discovered were not his brothers but his aged parents. In describing the watery lumper potato from the days of the Famine, Nixy called it "as old as fog." Up the road, Johnny, bent-backed in his blackened forge, had hammered metal since the age of fourteen: horseshoes, garden tables, ornate estate gates, you named it and he'd make it. Johnny insisted on charging ridiculously low prices and, though normally sweet-tempered, was indignant if anyone tried to pay more than he asked. Tight-fisted farmers were saddened when Johnny closed his forge to care for his ailing wife.

One rain-lashed night I glanced out a window and saw a dark figure stalking the muddy lane like a distraught Victorian heroine. Around midnight we heard a knock. Bernadette had got up courage to cadge a smoke. She came knocking every now and then after that, seeking a cigarette or a drink of water but never had much to say. On Sunday mornings we saw her in best dress and nylons, puffing on a fag and going up the lane to the house of the bachelor farmer. A single mother in her thirties who habitually walked eight miles into Wexford Town and eight miles back in an afternoon, she had a red-haired, teenage daughter whose wedding to the elderly milkman caused comment. People said Bernadette herself had once been pretty but had been "abused by men," for behind the tourist posters of quaint villages and cosy pubs lurked a darker Ireland of alcoholism, domestic violence, suicides and, recently, drugs. The pub-keeper up the road, a friendly, sociable man, turned violent and died of drink. Most suicides were young men, though an elderly neighbour who had kept his cows in our field was found hanging in his barn one morning having lived too long with untreated depression.

Among the farmers, the Travellers or Tinkers who came around were targets of scorn. One of our friends had arranged for Travellers to tarmac a driveway and then gone on a trip, leaving her son to supervise. Having started to pour tar near the house, they soon disappeared around a bend in her long, winding driveway. At day's end her son looked out the window, saw the smooth new tarmac and paid them at the door and bade them goodbye. Only after the Travellers had departed did he stroll down that evening to find they had laid tarmac no farther than the first bend.

Ignoring such cautionary tales I contracted with a Traveller to paint the exterior of our white house. The man seemed competent, but the motley crew he sent consisted of his frail-looking older brother Pat,

The Irish and Ireland, where we lived in the 1990s, gave us some of the happiest years of our lives.

plus an eighteen-year-old relative on crutches with a broken leg who did nothing but smoke cigarettes, and a hyperactive little boy of ten. During their first day I realized their white paint was of watery quality and the emaciated Pat with his graveyard cough would have to paint the whole house himself with neither safety harness nor insurance. I picked up a brush and began to paint with him, anything being better than sitting in the house and worrying that Pat might fall off the roof. We set the little boy to painting a fence out of harm's way. On the third and final day I was washing paint spatters from our car when the little boy suggested I clean Pat's car while I was at it. At that moment a bull with a bloody head charged through the open gate pursued by a farmer waving a bloody dehorning tool. Somehow the house got painted and Pat's car got washed.

I was back in Montreal when I got a long-distance call from the wife of a man building a house in a neighbouring field who asked me why she'd lost her electricity. It seemed odd she was phoning me in Canada about her Wexford electrical problems until she admitted that her husband, impatient to be connected to the power grid, had run a hundred feet of wire across the field to our house. Later I discovered that our protective friend Dick Shortall had driven over at midnight and snipped the illicit wire. They brought us a leg of lamb when we got back in the spring.

I remember the Irish as mostly a good-natured lot. One day in London a gang of Irish workmen had been tearing up Brixton Hill Road for the umpteenth time. Barbara had safely crossed in a lull of the traffic but was surprised to find I had suddenly disappeared like Alice down the rabbit hole. In starting across I had tumbled into one of the many roadside pits they were digging, only the top of my head showing above ground. Fortunately for me I had fallen on a workman from County Wexford, who not only broke my fall but whose reaction was one of concern for my welfare. "Sure, and can I help you out, sir?"

Less felicitous was the case of the disappearing well, which began when I turned on the tap and nothing came out. It had been a dry summer, our well was old and shallow. Out of curiosity and to please neighbours who believe in magic, I contacted a dowser, who divined a likely spot to drill where our property abutted an abandoned gravel pit. He urged me to try his forked sticks but they refused to move for me. Convinced that dowsing was nonsense and water was readily found in rainy Ireland, I hired more orthodox drillers. I should also have hired a geologist.

The drilling rig was as tall as our house and they could hardly get it through our gate. After a day and a half of boring through rock and bringing up muddy liquid, they got down to sixty feet and a sweet, clear flow of potable water. The problem then became getting the monster, mired in autumn muck, back out of our field. When a tractor failed, the two dispirited drill operators seemed ready to leave their giant contraption with us all winter until I discovered a farmer with a super-tractor big and powerful enough to haul the monster out, tearing up our property in the process.

For weeks we enjoyed clean cold water until a backhoe appeared one day in the neighbouring gravel pit just beyond our boundary hedge and our clean water turned yellow and smelled of rotten eggs. It seems the backhoe had somehow opened a vein of iron and an underground channel which was bleeding a sulphurous mix of iron and magnesium into our new $2,000 well. With no option but to return to our old well, I then discovered not only that there was sufficient water in it but that the problem had been simply clogged pipes.

In 1995 Barbara and I moved full time to an Ireland that was visibly changing. Mary Robinson, the first woman president, had become a popular liberal symbol and television was providing promise of cultural freedom and American consumerism. Church censorship was relaxed and divorce legalized and agriculture was losing its pride of place in the economy; the young were moving into towns and cities. Peace in Ulster after a quarter century of bloodshed was attracting investment. North American firms seeking an educated work force, favourable taxes, moderate wages and low costs shipping goods into the European market were launching the Republic into seven years of exceptional growth. Pharmaceutical, medical equipment, computer and software companies were opening branch plants in the have-not west, where Galway became the fastest-growing city in Europe. When we arrived in 1990 there had been far fewer homes in Moortown than there had been in the 18th century; now there were many more, new bungalows springing up, and "bungalow bliss" had become "bungalow blight."

In the late 1990s, as the *Economist* called Ireland "Europe's Shining Light," the unheard-of happened. A country that had been losing its youthful population for a century had become itself a destination for immigrants – from Poland, other parts of eastern Europe, Pakistan, India, even Africa. A land of white Roman Catholics was becoming multicultural and multiracial.

The cost was substantial. Though the Celtic Tiger produced a better quality of life for many, the pace and the longer work hours were causing stress and drug use and the poor and elderly were unable to keep up. In 2002 there were warnings the Celtic Tiger was losing its teeth, amid worries the country lacked the infrastructure to maintain such a pace. When the world economy collapsed in 2008, Ireland was once more a nation in economic distress.

Ireland had had a period of prosperity in which national income doubled; an inrush of capital created a brief illusion of wealth during which reckless banks made record loans to questionable borrowers. Charles Mackay's 1841 classic *Extraordinary Popular Delusions and the Madness of Crowds,* a cautionary history of market crazes and irrational fads, might have been written of 1990s Dublin as well as 1990s Wall Street.

Our decision to move back to Canada in 2001 had nothing to do with the economy. I was approaching the age of eighty and sooner or later would need more medical assistance and other urban amenities. Our first thought had been to move into Wexford Town but the cost of a suitable house had become prohibitive. Leaving came hard, but at the end of the year we sold up and departed for Canada, our lives enriched by Ireland, the people, the culture and the landscape.

The house at Moortown after a decade of building and gardening.

19

THE HILLS OF HOME

Framed in my window, Cape Blomidon floats between a blue autumnal sky and the silver tide flooding into Minas Basin from the Bay of Fundy. When the weather is poor the Cape turns grey. Today it is green, streaked with the rosy-red of its cliffs. Among the hills on the far shore is the place I was born.

Sheltered by North Mountain and the curving dikes that bar the sea, our Valley is a fruitful affinity of land and sea, the food basket of a land-poor province. Barbara and I have come to a tranquil university town named not for wolves, as I'd imagined as a child, but for Judge Elisha DeWolf, whose 19th-century nieces were embarrassed by the original name of Mud Creek, though it accurately described the chocolate colour of the tiny empty harbour when the mighty tides retreated.

In Elisha's day, creeks and inlets rang with the sound of yards building tall ships that carried Valley apples to the world. The shipyards are gone but within a short drive from our door there are fishing villages, salt marshes, five rivers, orchards and vineyards and Cape Split, where tides with the combined flow of all the world's rivers come rushing through from Fundy twice daily to replenish Minas Basin and carve little islands shaped like flower pots from the sandy red cliffs. Behind us between Wolfville Ridge and South Mountain delectable Gaspereau Valley leads to an upland wilderness of woods and lakes and the backbone of Nova Scotia.

Wide windows and open verandas flood our house with light, Barbara's garden has progressed through the seasons from snowdrops to black-eyed Susans – a palette of red, blue, pink, yellow and white.

There are crows, chickadees, swifts, robins, blackbirds and patriotic white-throated sparrows who sing "O sweet Canada, Canada, Canada," observed from the window by Hamish, our grey and white tabby. We are surrounded by trees – conifers, birch, elm, lilac, apple. The land below our hillside home falls steeply through blueberry bushes into an overgrown ravine populated by a noisy family of pheasants, sly raccoons and unseen squirrels who steal insulation for their nests from under the hood of our Toyota Corolla.

I now am of an age when time sweeps us into an unfamiliar world. Things we used to be quick at doing take longer. We tend to avoid the mirror. When I was much younger I had imagined old age magically rendered people sagacious and serene, though I now find I am really the same person I have always been. Horizons shrink and friends disappear but hope and curiosity remain. "Eighty years old!" wrote the poet Paul Claudel. "No eyes, no ears, no teeth no legs, no

Barbara's Wolfville cottage garden, where perennial flowers, as informal, diverse and charming as the devoted gardener, come and go with the seasons.

wind, and how astonishing well one does without them." An old man's jest. But while we do not always succeed in greeting old age with dignity and humour there are pleasures. The other day Barbara and I hiked along Nova Scotia's South Shore with our daughters, here on their annual visit, Karen from England, Marina from her quinta in the hills of southwest Spain. Our destination was the coastal Kejimkujik National Park; a perfect day of Atlantic vistas, white sand beaches, rocky promontories, birds, mammals, reptiles, seals, whales and rare species once common to the whole province but now found only in this small South Shore peninsula.

One of the advantages of old age, it's been argued, is that you get to see what happened, meaning I suppose that a long life ideally provides perspective, reveals truths, sorts the significant from the trivial. But no one, however lucky, lives long enough to witness more than a few acts, never the whole play. We are undone by the lacunae between the act and the recollection, by cues missed and scenes forgotten. Time becomes skewed. When I was young the Edwardians and Victorians and World War I were ancient history, people and events in books and fading photos. Only when my own years began to

PHOTOGRAPH BY STEPHEN SLIPP

Wolfville, with Acadia University in the background, seen from the dikes.

JOE DELANEY

The traveller at rest.

mount up did it strike me that the Great War had ended only seven years before I was born and Kipling and Hardy were alive when I was a child.

We are all bridges in time and I was born in a simpler age before talking movies, rampant consumerism, ubiquitous automobiles and television; long before astronauts broached our Old Testament heaven, walked on the moon and described our vulnerable little world as a shimmering blue sphere in an ocean of black space. During my eighty-five years the shrinking world has suffered shock after shock – the Great Depression, World War II, the deliberate bombing of cities full of civilians, the Holocaust, the atomic bombing of Japan, famines, the Cold War, Vietnam, wars and more wars, in Iraq and Afghanistan and elsewhere. I recall VE-Day, 1945, when people expressed the wish, even the certainty, the world was about to get better. In the 1950s I heard Sir Winston Churchill say, "The leading men of various nations should be able to meet together, without trying to cut attitudes before excitable publics … let us see if there is not something better for all than tearing and blasting each other to pieces." In the end, our 20th century turned out to be the most destructive century in history, with estimates of 100 million killed in wars, famines, genocides and other disasters. Two millennia since the pre-Christian Axis Age began to transform the world by planting the monotheistic seeds of the world's great religions, we remain unable to create effective antidotes to human inhumanity and unjustified war. The world government Churchill envisaged is beyond our grasp.

"The story of your life is not your life, it is your story," wrote John Barth. Recalled in words and images our memoirs are diluted or enhanced with emotion and imagination. Yet many of us are tempted to seek meaningful patterns in the random days of our lives. Having lived through much of the 20th century reporting on the lives and times of others, this is my own story.

Karen and Marina at Kejimkujik National Park.

INDEX

Index

Marquis Book Printing Inc.

Québec, Canada
2010